The Lifespan
of a Fact

The Lifespan of a Fact

John D'Agata and Jim Fingal

W. W. Norton & Company

NEW YORK · LONDON

For information about permission to reproduce selections from this book, write to
Permissions, W. W. Norton & Company, Inc., 500 Fifth Avenue, New York, NY 10110

For information about special discounts for bulk purchases, please contact
W. W. Norton Special Sales at specialsales@wwnorton.com or 800-233-4830

Manufacturing by LSC Harrisonburg
Book design by Chris Welch
Production manager: Anna Oler

Library of Congress Cataloging-in-Publication Data

D'Agata, John, 1974–
The lifespan of a fact / John D'Agata and Jim Fingal. — 1st ed.
p. cm.
Includes bibliographical references.
ISBN 978-0-393-34073-0 (pbk.)
1. Creative nonfiction—Authorship. 2. Essay—Authorship. I. Fingal, Jim. II. Title.
PN145.D25 2012
808.02–dc23

2011042637

W. W. Norton & Company, Inc.
500 Fifth Avenue, New York, N.Y. 10110
www.wwnorton.com

W. W. Norton & Company Ltd.
15 Carlisle Street, London W1D 3BS

7 8 9 0

True words are not beautiful.

—*Lao-tzu*

Beautiful words are not true.

—Lao-tzu

The Lifespan
of a Fact

From the Editor:

I've got a fun assignment for somebody. We just received a
new piece from John D'Agata that needs to be fact-checked,
thoroughly. Apparently he's taken some liberties, which he's
admitted to, but I want to know to what extent. So whoever's
up for it will need to comb through this, marking anything
and everything that you can confirm as true, as well as
whatever you think is questionable. I'll buy you a pack of red
pens if necessary.

Thanks!

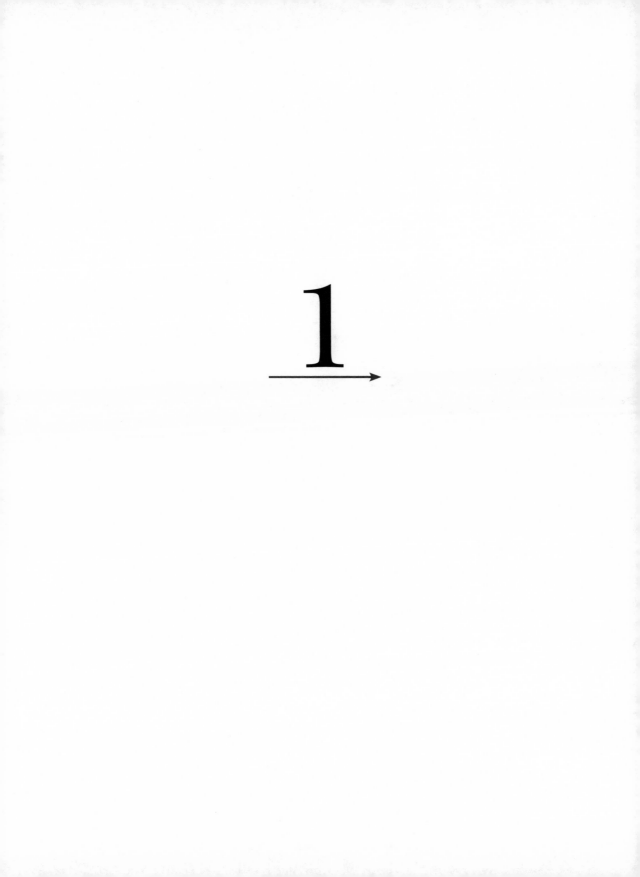

1

"On the same day in Las Vegas when sixteen-year-old Levi Presley . . ." The age and name of the deceased can be confirmed by the county's official Coroner's Report, dated July 13, 2002.

". . . jumped from the observation deck . . ." Confirmed by the same Coroner's Report, explaining that Presley descended from an "observation deck" at the Stratosphere Hotel and Casino.

". . . 1,149-foot-high tower of the Stratosphere Hotel and Casino . . ." Name and height of the tower confirmed on the Stratosphere's website.

". . . lap dancing was temporarily banned by the city . . ." Factual Dispute: *The Las Vegas Sun* published an article on July 12, the day preceding Levi Presley's death, which referred to a *possible* ban against touching strippers enforced throughout the city, although at that point the ban hadn't taken effect, as reported by Erin Neff in "Political Notebook," *Las Vegas Sun,* July 12, 2002. So John's claim here isn't technically accurate.

". . . in thirty-four licensed strip clubs in Vegas . . ." Factual Dispute: Not sure where John got this number from. The only reference I can find in his notes to the number of strip clubs that exist in Las Vegas is from a photocopy of an article he provided from a publication entitled *Adult Industry News,* which is a newsletter for the porn industry. So the source of his information is a little suspicious to begin with. Nevertheless, the article mentions that since 1995 "the number of strip clubs [in Las Vegas] has skyrocketed from three to sixteen." But then it goes on to also claim that there are "thirty-one topless or all-nude clubs" ("Vegas Sex Industry Fights Gov't Crackdown on Lap Dances" by Angie Wagner, *Adult Industry News,* January 3, 2003). So even if we trusted the source and its self-contradiction, John's claim of thirty-four strip clubs still isn't supported by this article. And even if that number were supported by the article, there's still the issue of the article's authority, given that it itself offers two contradictory numbers. So, should I ask him to clarify this number?

Editor: Sure, go ahead and ask him for a little more help in tracking the number down.

. . .

Jim: Hi, John. I'm Jim Fingal, I'm the intern who's been assigned to fact-check your article about Las Vegas, and I've discovered a small discrepancy between the number of strip clubs you're claiming there are in Las Vegas and the number that's given in your supporting documents. I'm new at this, so bear with me. I was hoping that you could clarify how you determined that there are thirty-four strip clubs in the city while the source you're using says thirty-one.

John: Hi, Jim. I think maybe there's some sort of miscommunication, because the "article," as you call it, is fine. It shouldn't need a fact-checker; at least that was my understanding with the editor I've been working with. I have taken some liberties in the essay here and there, but none of them are harmful. And I've actually been assuming that everyone was cool with what I turned in. But I've also given the magazine all of my research so that people there could see for themselves what I was up to when I took these liberties. So I'm not sure it's going to be worth your time to fact-check this. I've been open about all such "discrepancies."

Jim: I hear you. But I think it's just policy to fact-check all the nonfiction pieces the magazine publishes. Plus it's the job I was assigned to do, so I have to do it. I've also already made a trip out there to check up on a few things in the essay because my friend was getting married and I knew this assignment was coming up. (Penn and Teller say hi BTW!) So I've made a bit of an investment in this myself. But really I think they just want to make sure that all the facts in the piece add up, especially since there are a lot of them and your claims sometimes get a little inflammatory. (In a good way of course . . . =)) So could you help me out with that number?

John: Inflammatory?

Jim: I mean in a hard-hitting and intriguing way. Wrong choice of words, sorry!

John: All right. Well, from what I can remember, I

O n the same day in Las Vegas when sixteen-year-old Levi Presley jumped from the observation deck of the 1,149-foot-high tower of the Stratosphere Hotel and Casino, lap dancing was temporarily banned by the city in thirty-four

got that number by counting up the number of strip clubs that were listed in the local yellow pages at the time of Levi's death. However, since that issue of the phone book was long gone by the time I started writing this, I found that porn article that I gave the magazine so that they could check up on my estimate.

Jim: Thanks, John. Very helpful. Now, I guess that's where the discrepancy is, because the number that's mentioned in the article is different from the number you're using in your piece.

John: Well, I guess that's because the rhythm of "thirty-four" works better in that sentence than the rhythm of "thirty-one," so I changed it.

Jim: Ah. OK. Well thanks for your time, John, I'll probably be checking back with you later on.

. . .

So, do we accept that?

Editor: Not his "rhythm" explanation, but his procedure for estimating that number is fine. Just try to confirm in the yellow pages that thirty-four was accurate in 2002.

Jim: Well, unless you want me to fly back to Las Vegas in order to track down a 2002 copy of the yellow pages, all I can use is the current online directory, which can't really indicate one way or the other the status of strip clubs in 2002. The current edition says that there are now twenty-nine strip clubs in town, so unless the number rose and then dropped again, there's likely a factual discrepancy here.

Editor: OK, Jim. Then just note the discrepancy and move on.

". . . archaeologists unearthed parts of the world's oldest bottle of Tabasco-brand sauce from underneath a bar called Buckets of Blood . . ." Factual Dispute: This happened on June 28, 2002, fifteen days before Levi Presley killed himself, so it wasn't discovered the same day he died. In addition, the bottle was discovered in Virginia City, which is 20 miles southeast of Reno—about 450 miles away from Las Vegas. So the relevance of this bottle's discovery to Las Vegas is a little specious. Also, the bar it was found under is called the "Boston Saloon," which, as the *Las Vegas Review-Journal* reported, is "behind the

licensed strip clubs in Vegas, archaeologists unearthed parts of the world's oldest bottle of Tabasco-brand sauce from underneath a bar called Buckets of Blood, and a woman from Mississippi beat a chicken named Ginger in a thirty-five-minute-long game of tic-tac-toe.

Bucket of Blood Saloon." The point being that none of this corresponds in any way with Levi Presley's death. ("Hot Sauce Bottle Used in 1870s Found" by Scott Sonner, *Las Vegas Review-Journal,* June 28, 2002.) What should I do here?

Editor: Go ahead and ask him about this, too.

. . .

Jim: John, I discovered that the bar you mention in the beginning of your piece where they found that Tabasco sauce bottle is actually called the "Boston Saloon." Do you want to change it?

John: No, why would I change it? "Bucket of Blood" is more interesting than the "Boston Saloon," and since they found it near the Bucket of Blood, I think the claim is OK as it stands. From what I understand, you are fact-checking this, right, not editing it?

. . .

Jim: Any suggestion on what to do here?

Editor: Just note it and move on, Jim. We'll deal with the discrepancies later.

". . . and a woman from Mississippi beat a chicken named Ginger in a thirty-five-minute-long game of tic-tac-toe." Factual Dispute: According to the press release John provided from the hotel where this took place, this tic-tac-toe game actually happened on August 13, 2002, a full month after Levi Presley's death. Plus, while the woman who won the match was originally from Mississippi, she was actually a resident of Las Vegas when the game happened. So . . . ?

Editor: All right, ask him.

. . .

Jim: Hey, John . . . again =). I was wondering if you could weigh in on this tic-tac-toe game with the chicken. It looks like it happened quite a bit after Levi Presley died, but also that the woman who won it wasn't really from Mississippi. I think she was a local resident. Does this matter?

John: I realize that, but I need her to be from a place other than Las Vegas in order to underscore the transient nature of the city—that nearly everyone in Vegas is from someplace else. And since she did in fact originally come from Mississippi, I think the claim is fine as it is.

Jim: What about that fact that this didn't occur on the day Presley died? It's not accurate to say that it did.

John: It was part of the atmosphere of that particular summer.

Jim: Then isn't that how it should be framed so that it is more accurate?

John: No, because being more precise would be less dramatic and would sound a lot clunkier. I don't think readers will care whether the events that I'm discussing happened on the same day, a few days apart, or a few months apart. What most readers will care about, I think, is the meaning that's suggested in the confluence of these events—no matter how far apart they occurred. The facts that are being employed here aren't meant to function baldly as "facts." The work that they're doing is more image-based than informational. Nobody is going to read this, in other words, in order to get a survey of the demographics of Las Vegas or what's scheduled on the community calendar. Readers can get that kind of information elsewhere.

. . .

Jim: For a piece that seems to rest on the weight of a lot of details, it seems a little problematic for John to be washing his hands of their accuracy, no?

Editor: Just stay on track with the fact-checking, Jim. I'll figure out in the end which inaccuracies are acceptable.

Jim: We're only one sentence into his piece, though, and I don't think this is the worst of it.

Editor: Don't worry. How 'bout you just work with John directly from now on? It'll save time if you don't have to check back with me on every problem you encounter. I'm here if any questions come up, though. Just be thorough, and question whatever you think is problematic, respectfully.

Jim: Alrighty.

". . . five others died from two types of cancer . . ." I can confirm this based on an email John received from a secretary at the Coroner's Office, dated August 12, 2002.

". . . four from heart attacks . . ." Factual Dispute: According to the Coroner's Office, there were two

heart attacks that day. But besides these two particular coronary cases handled by the Coroner's Office, there were an additional five cardiorespiratory arrests and one additional myocardial infarction which were never investigated by the Coroner's Office, presumably because they took place in hospitals. So there were actually eight "heart attacks" that day, not four.

John, should we change this "four heart attacks" to "eight"?

John: I like the effect of these numbers scaling down in the sentence from five to four to three, etc. So I'd like to leave it as is.

Jim: But that would be intentionally inaccurate.

John: Probably, yeah.

Jim: Aren't you worried about your credibility with the reader?

John: Not really, Jim, no. I'm not running for public office. I'm trying to write something that's interesting to read.

Jim: But what's the point if the reader stops trusting you?

John: The readers who care about the difference between "four" and "eight" might stop trusting me. But the readers who care about interesting sentences and the metaphorical effect that the accumulation of those sentences achieve will probably forgive me.

Jim: I guess I'm confused: what exactly are the benefits of using "four" versus "eight" in this sentence?

John: I'm done talking about this.

". . . three because of strokes." Confirmed: email from Coroner's Office, August 12, 2002.

"It was a day of two suicides by gunshot as well." According to Sheri Renaud at the Clark County Coroner's Office, there were indeed two suicides that were the result of self-inflicted gunshots.

"The day of yet another suicide from hanging." Factual Dispute: But according to Ms. Renaud, the third additional suicide that occurred that day was also the result of someone jumping off a building, not from hanging.

John, can you clarify?

> **On the day that Levi Presley died, five others died from two types of cancer, four from heart attacks, three because of strokes.**
>
> **It was a day of two suicides by gunshot as well.**
>
> **The day of yet another suicide from hanging.**

John: Yeah, I think I remember changing this because I wanted Levi's death to be the only one from falling that day. I wanted his death to be more unique.

. . .

Jim: OK, I know I'm just an intern here, but "I wanted his death to be more unique"?

Editor: Jim, just note it. Move on. We'll deal with it. I can't referee every problem you have with the piece. John's a different kind of writer, so you are going to encounter some irregularities in the project. Just keep your report as thorough as possible and we'll comb through it all later.

Jim: But every writer is "different"—does this mean that he's getting a special dispensation from the magazine's fact-checking policies, which you guys so thoroughly drilled into us?

Editor: Not necessarily, no. But it means that we're going to have to deal with the irregularities of this piece with an open mind.

"At a record 118 degrees, it also happened to be one of that summer's hottest days . . ." Factual Dispute: According to *Vegas.com*, the "Official Las Vegas Travel Site," the hottest day ever recorded in Las Vegas was on July 24, 1942, which registered at only at 117 degrees F. The temperature for the day Levi died was 113 degrees F, according to the statistics of the website *Weather Underground*. However, according to that same website, 113 degrees was still the hottest day of the year, so it was "a record" of sorts.

". . . a day that caused the World's Tallest Thermometer to break . . ." Factual Dispute: The World's Tallest Thermometer is located in Baker, California, on the road between Barstow and Vegas. It's actually officially known as the World's Largest Thermometer to be precise, so while it technically is also the "tallest," the name John is giving the thermometer is a little misleading. It's a 134-foot electric sign erected to memorialize the temperature

At a record 118 degrees, it also happened to be one of that summer's hottest days—a day that caused the World's Tallest Thermometer to break, raised the price of bottled water to five dollars for eight ounces, and caused a traffic jam on the north end of the Las Vegas Strip as a tourist family traveled toward downtown Las Vegas, rolled over a broken bottle from a homeless woman's cart, blew out a back tire, hit a parked car, and stalled outside the entrance of the Stratosphere Hotel when the jack inside the back of their rented Dodge Stratus sank into the heat-softened asphalt of the street.

on July 10, 1913, which was a record 134 degrees F in Death Valley, 150 miles from Vegas. All I can find regarding its breaking is a report that states that at one point early in its existence the thermometer fell down due to strong winds. I can't find anything to confirm that it was broken the day Presley died, however. Also, it seems unlikely that an electric sign would break due to a high temperature—it's not like its electrons would overboil or something. Therefore, even if for some reason it was broken that day, the statement of causation seems bogus.

". . . raised the price of bottled water to five dollars for eight ounces . . ." Factual Dispute: This level of granularity about something as ephemeral as what a street vendor would charge for a bottle of water is pretty hard to check, so I'm not sure what I can say about this. I can't find any news articles that mention this fact, and John doesn't have any notes to confim it. However, I can say that I'm pretty sure that most major water producers stick to 12, 16.9, or 20 ounce sizes. I'm a little suspicious therefore of this "eight ounce" claim.

". . . and caused a traffic jam on the north end of the Las Vegas Strip as a tourist family traveled toward downtown Las Vegas, rolled over a broken bottle from a homeless woman's cart, blew out a back tire, hit a parked car, and stalled outside the entrance of the Stratosphere Hotel when the jack inside the back of their rented Dodge Stratus sank into the heat-softened asphalt of the street." Factual Dispute: There's no mention of this accident in the archives of either the *Las Vegas Review-Journal* or the *Las Vegas Sun*, the two major papers in the city.

John, do you have a source for this?

John: I heard about this from a woman I interviewed at the Aztec Inn, which is across the street from the Stratosphere. The day after Levi's death, I began some casual research in the neighborhood surrounding the Stratosphere. The woman claimed that she witnessed not only Levi's fall but also the traffic jam that preceded it.

Jim: Can you send me a copy of your notes from this interview?

John: I didn't keep notes from the interview. I probably noted what this woman said by jotting down something like "homeless lady" and "traffic accident," but beyond that I just relied on my memory of what she told me. Besides, this wasn't a formal interview. At this point I was just wandering around the Stratosphere trying to gather information. I didn't even know if I was going to write about Levi.

Jim: To be honest, I suspect your "casual" interviewing strategy is going to be a problem, because it means that we're not going to have anything that can remotely come close to proving what you've written.

John: Well it might be a problem, but with all due respect, it's your problem, Jim, not mine. I'm not a reporter, and I have never claimed to be a reporter, and the magazine took on this project with the understanding that I have no interest in pretending to be a reporter or in producing journalism. Also, even if this had been a formal interview, I still wouldn't have taken extensive notes, because I tend to be casual whenever I'm interviewing people so that they feel more comfortable with me. The minute you take out a tape recorder or a notebook during an interview people get self-conscious and start "performing" for you, watching what they say and how they say it. So when I interview someone it's usually over lunch or a drink or during a walk or something. When people think they're in a conversation as opposed to an interview they are much more relaxed and thus more forthcoming.

Jim: Well, OK . . . I guess . . . but this still seems to violate about ten different rules of journalistic integrity.

John: I'm not sure that matters, Jim. This is an essay, so journalistic rules don't belong here.

Jim: I'm not sure it's going to be quite that easy.

"We therefore know that when Levi Presley jumped from the tower of the Stratosphere Hotel at 6:01:43 p.m.—eventually hitting the ground at 6:01:52 p.m. . . ." Factual Dispute: Although the incident did happen at "18:01," according to the Coroner's Report, Levi Presely's fall supposedly only took eight seconds,

not nine. So the actual time frame would be more like "6:01:43–6:01:51."

John?

John: Yeah, I fudged that. It doesn't seem like it should be that big a deal, though. It's only a second. And I needed him to fall for nine seconds rather than eight in order to help make some of the later themes in the essay work.

Jim: John, changing details about stuff like Tabasco sauce bottles and thermometers is one thing, but it seems a tad unethical to fiddle with details that relate directly to this kid's death. In my book, it just seems wrong, especially since the coroner clearly states that Presley's fall only took eight seconds.

John: I don't think it's unethical, particularly because I wasn't alone in assuming that his fall took nine seconds. For a while his parents also assumed that he had fallen for nine seconds. In fact, that's where I initially got the number from. Do you think I'd just change this willy-nilly to suit some sort of literary trick I wanted to pull off? His parents and I had a fairly explicit conversation about these nine seconds with Levi's old Tae Kwon Do coach. So with that little bit of information, I began thinking about some of the ways that the number nine could play a thematic role in the essay.

Jim: OK, I'll grant you that at one point you didn't know the correct number, but now you do know better, so shouldn't it change?

John: "Nine" is too integral a part of the essay at this point. And I admit that I'm wrong about "nine" later on anyway. So the essay's not changing. It would ruin the essay.

Jim: It would "ruin" it to make it more accurate?

John: Yup.

". . . there were over a hundred tourists in five dozen cars that were honking and bumping and idling and yelling . . ." Epistemological Problem: This assertion must be rampant speculation, unless someone was actually at the scene of this accident counting the number of people who were in these cars. In any case, there were probably a lot more than a hundred people at this scene if this was an actual "traffic jam." At that intersection, which is a T intersection (Baltimore Avenue comes in from the west and dead-ends into Las Vegas Boulevard), there are six lanes on Las Vegas,

> We therefore know that when Levi Presley jumped from the tower of the Stratosphere Hotel at 6:01:43 p.m.—eventually hitting the ground at 6:01:52 p.m.—there were over a hundred tourists in five dozen cars that were honking

and four on Baltimore. So the "five dozen cars" that John notes only comes out to about sixty cars. If we spread that number out across each segment of road that feeds into this intersection—with about a third of the cars on each of the three segments of the T—this comes to only about five cars in each lane going to or from the intersection on Baltimore Avenue and three cars in each lane going to or from the intersection on Las Vegas Boulevard. Now, even if all sixty of these cars were on Las Vegas Boulevard at the exact same spot where Levi hit the ground, that would still only be ten cars in each lane of the street (an average of twelve feet per car would equal less than 150 feet of congestion). When I was there at 6 p.m. on a Saturday night, there were probably at least this many cars in the immediate area, with no accident in sight. So I very much doubt John's estimate. In fact, there's a constant level of baseline traffic nearly everywhere in Las Vegas. According to the website *Guide to Vegas,* heavy traffic is a given there. That website's advice to tourists, in fact, is to "avoid driving on Las Vegas Boulevard (the Strip). Instead, use Paradise to the east and Industrial to the west as much as possible. Personally speaking, 26 miles of the 405 in Southern California every day for a year was never as bad as Strip traffic on an early Friday night." So, in my estimation, there would probably be upwards of two hundred vehicles in that intersection at the time, which would actually be—if we allowed an average of 1.6 people per car—six hundred people in the kind of massive traffic jam John's purporting, although I freely admit that that's something of a wild guess. John, could you clarify?

John: The woman at the Aztec Inn said that there were about five dozen cars there. That should be enough for us.

". . . at the base of the Stratosphere tower." Possible Dispute: I guess this depends on how you define "at the base of" the tower. The base of the tower itself is several yards away from this intersection. The tower is not, in other words, right at the intersection. The main driveway to the casino is immediately to your left as you're traveling north up Las Vegas Boulevard; only

and bumping and idling and yelling at the base of the Stratosphere tower.

Some of them looked up from the traffic jam that night and briefly saw in the sky something fall from the dark, and then through the palms, and then to the city's pavement. Some of them left their cars to look down at what had

if you keep going fifty feet or so—onto the sidewalk and a small pavilion in front of the hotel—will you get to what is actually the "base" of the tower. So "near the base" of the tower is probably more accurate. John, do you want to change this?

John: Nope. "At the base" is sharper-sounding and more precise.

Jim: But it's inaccurate. How could it be more precise?

John: It sounds more pointed, and thus more accurate, and that therefore gives the sentence a feeling of greater precision and authority. "Near the base" sounds wishy-washy, just as if I rewrote the opening sentence of the essay to read "Within the same basic time frame as Levi Presley's death . . ."

"Some of them looked up from the traffic jam that night and briefly saw in the sky something fall from the dark, and then through the palms, and then to the city's pavement. Some of them left their cars to look down at what had fallen." Epistemological Problem: "tourists." Since the official witness statements about this incident haven't been released (see below), and considering that John wasn't actually there to hear people talking about the incident, this seems like speculation. Also, as is later stated in the essay and confirmed in the Coroner's Report, Levi landed on the hotel's driveway, not "the sidewalk." And besides, the sidewalk surrounding the Stratosphere is brick, not "pavement." So really none of this is accurate. Another issue: the Stratosphere is surrounded by many palm trees—they line the sidewalk and surround the driveway—so someone watching from across the street might indeed have had their vision of Presley's fall obstructed by the palm trees, but they certainly didn't see his fall partially broken by said trees. In other words, they would have "seen him fall, through the palm trees" vs. "seen him 'fall through the palm trees.'" John's garden-pathy sentence is confusing, and should probably be amended.

John: I'm sorry, I don't know what any of that means. Just leave it as is.

"And ten of them gave statements . . ." The Coroner's Report lists a total of only six witness statements, although only two of those six are noted as actual "bystanders." John's own notes from his conversation with the police officer also reference that the "report has six witness statements." John himself interviewed another four people who claimed to have witnessed the incident, but their statements aren't "official" because they weren't introduced into the police record or the Coroner's Report. So I think John's a little confused here.

"'You don't want to read any of that, man. That stuff is just facts. None of this is gonna sound like a Mickey Spillane novel. You know?'" Possible Alteration: The actual quote that appears in John's notes from this guy is "All I can tell you is what's public—it'll be sanitized—it's not going to sound like a Mickey Spillane novel." The "facts" part of that sentence seems to be an insertion by John. Also, it looks like he changed this officer's name (is that allowed?), since I can't find a "Steve Barela" listed with the Las Vegas Police Department. There is a Rick Barela, however, according to a search of the local papers ("Las Vegas Police Officer Arrested after Scuffle," *Las Vegas Review-Journal,* June 30, 2004).
John: I punched up his statement, but I think the basic gist is the same.
Jim: "Punched up"?

"When I asked a woman at Las Vegas Teen Crisis whether suicide is a problem for teenagers in the city, she told me that she preferred I 'not write any of that down.'" Factual Dispute: I can't find this quote anywhere in John's notes. Even then, if this is the same

fallen. And ten of them gave statements of what they saw to the police.

When I asked the Las Vegas Metropolitan Police Department whether I could read some of those statements that the witnesses had given, Police Sergeant Steve Barela explained, "You don't want to read any of that, man. That stuff is just facts. None of this is gonna sound like a Mickey Spillane novel. You know?"

When I asked a woman at Las Vegas Teen Crisis whether suicide is a problem for teenagers in the city, she told me that she preferred I "not write any of that down."

When I asked Michael Gilmartin, the public relations manager at the Stratosphere Hotel, whether his hotel has a system in place for discouraging people from jumping off his tall tower, first he asked me if I was kidding, and then he said, "Listen, I don't want to be associated with some piece about a kid who

woman who appears in John's notes elsewhere, what she's saying seems to contradict what she stated about the importance of being forthcoming about suicide in a *Las Vegas Review-Journal* article: "'People don't talk about suicide. There's this stigma attached to it,' she said. 'But we have a serious problem in Nevada. We lead the nation in suicides every year. We're not going to eradicate it, but with better awareness, maybe we can help slow it down'" ("Suicide of Son Gives Mom's Life a New Meaning" by Richard Lake, *Las Vegas Review-Journal,* December 1, 2002). So that sentiment is quite clearly the exact opposite of what John's attributing to her here.

John: How would you know if this is the same woman as the one I'm talking about? I changed this woman's identity. As far as I know, "Las Vegas Teen Crisis" doesn't even exist.
Jim: Because I'm very good at my job.
John: So good that you know the employees of nonexistent organizations?
Jim: Good enough to be able to figure out what you're up to.

". . . first he asked if I was kidding, and then he said, 'Listen, I don't want to be associated with some piece about a kid who killed himself here, OK? I mean, really, what's the upside to that? All I can see is a downside. If you can tell me how this story could benefit the hotel, then maybe we could discuss it, but right now I don't want to be a part of it.'" Alteration of Quote: In John's notes, the actual quote from Gilmartin reads: "I just don't want to be associated in any way, shape, or form with a piece about someone killing themselves. I mean, what's the upside to that? All I see is a downside." Another Alteration: Gilmartin's official title at the Stratosphere is the "vice president of public relations," according to a press release I found, although his title could have changed since 2002. Also, this part of the essay seems to be told from the point of view of the present looking back, so maybe we should refer to him as the "public relations manager at the time"?

John: No, that's ridiculously clunky. Leave it alone. And please don't offer to do any more writing for me, thank you.

"What I know for certain about Levi Presley is what he looked like, how old he was, what kind of car he drove, what school he attended, what girl he liked and what girl liked him, his favorite outfit, favorite movie, favorite restaurant, favorite band, what level belt he held in Tae Kwon Do, what design he had sketched onto the wall of his bedroom— very lightly, in pencil— and later planned to fill in, which drawings of his from art school he is thought to have been particularly proud of and whether their themes could be said to provide an indication of suicidal 'ideation,' the nickname of his car, the two different nicknames his parents had each given him . . ." Query to John: I know you're not a journalist, but are your notes from these interviews with Levi's

killed himself here, OK? I mean, really, what's the upside to that? All I can see is a downside. If you can tell me how this story could benefit the hotel, then maybe we could discuss it, but right now I don't want to be a part of it."

What I know for certain about Levi Presley is what he looked like, how old he was, what kind of car he drove, what school he attended, what girl he liked and what girl liked him, his favorite outfit, favorite movie, favorite restaurant, favorite band, what level belt he held in Tae Kwon Do, what design he had sketched onto the wall of his bedroom—very lightly, in pencil—and later planned to fill in, which drawings of his from art school he is thought to have been particularly proud of and whether their themes could be said to provide an indication of suicidal "ideation," the nickname of his car, the two different nicknames his parents had each given

I'm doing these kinds of interviews. That's probably nontraditional or even unprofessional, but since it took me about three months to get Levi's parents to agree to meet with me, I wasn't willing to jeopardize that by bringing in a tape recorder or a notebook and intimidating them. So, except for the interviews I did for "fact-gathering" with the police or the coroner, the interviews that were conducted with real people tended to be unrecorded. Again, this is because I think that most people aren't used to being interviewed and so they don't know how to relax during the process—the result being that everything they say sounds canned. Therefore, with Levi's parents I gathered information slowly over a period of about two weeks, driving around with them in their car, hanging out with them in their home, eating dinner with them, watching TV with them, visiting Levi's old dojo, looking over his art, chatting with his friends, etc. I doubt that most "nonfiction" writers and readers would approve of this way of gathering information because it isn't "nonfictionally" verifiable, but I don't care. I'm tired of this genre being terrorized by an unsophisticated reading public that's afraid of accidentally venturing into terrain that can't be

parents in a different notebook other than the ones you gave me? In the notebooks you gave me there appears to be one short phone conversation with Levi's mom, and then a couple of one-liners from his dad. Can the rest of this be found elsewhere? Information from the Presleys is a big chunk of the factual material in this piece, so I would like to be able to verify as much of it as possible.

John: As I've told you, Jim, I don't take notes when

footnoted and verified by seventeen different sources. My job is not to re-create a world that already exists, holding up a mirror to the reader's experience in hopes that it rings true. If a mirror were a sufficient means of handling human experience, I doubt that our species would have invented literature.

Jim: Note to self: John is not a journalist. Also not a nonfiction writer. He is, however, a writer of journalistic-ish texts that are not necessarily fiction. Got it.

"*. . . his answers to the questions on the last pop quiz he took in school—What is good? What is bad? What does "art" mean to you? Now look at the chair on the table in front of you and describe it in literal terms . . .*" Confirmed: "What is bad" and "What is good" are indeed sections in the test that John's describing, as is "What does 'art' mean to you." But there's an inconsistency in a part of the quote. The exact question on the test is "Look at the chair placed on the table in front of you. Describe this chair, literally (what does it look like?)." Another dispute: These questions are taken from an "Art Pretest," rather than what John is calling a "pop quiz." If my memory of high school serves me correctly, pre-tests are worksheets you do before a test in order to help you study for it, and this is corroborated by the fact that there is no grade on this pretest. So it would be inaccurate to call this a "pop quiz." And finally: The test is dated August 25, 1999, and Levi's death was on July 12, 2002, so even if this were a "pop quiz," it's very unlikely that it was "the last pop quiz he took in school," unless he was one lucky kid.

John: OK, you're probably right that this wasn't his "last" quiz. But it's more dramatic to say that it was, and I don't think it's harming anyone to do that. It's not like there's a quiz out there that'll get jealous if we claim that this was Levi's last quiz. Really, Jim, respectfully, you're worrying about very stupid shit. (By the way, also very stupid would be calling this quiz a "pretest," because I kind of suspect that half the readers out there wouldn't even know what the fuck that was.)

Jim: Unfortunately I don't get to decide which facts are stupid; I have to check all of them. Although I admit that it would certainly save me a lot of time with this essay if I were allowed to make that distinction.

---

him, his answers to the questions on the last pop quiz he took in school—

What is good? What is bad? What does "art" mean to you? Now look at the chair on the table in front of you and describe it in literal terms

—and of which bottle of cologne among the five Levi kept in the medicine cabinet down the hall his small bedroom still smelled, even after his parents had ripped up its carpeting, thrown out its bed, and emptied its closet of everything but his art, by the time I first visited them, three months after his death.

What I know for certain about Levi Presley, in other words, is whatever Gail, his mom, and Levi Senior, his dad, were willing to say to a person they'd never met before about their sixteen-year-old son, which was, I quickly realized upon meeting them, anything.

"Whatever you want," they said. "We'll go on the record about anything."

"*. . . and of which bottle of cologne among the five Levi kept in the medicine cabinet down the hall his small bedroom still smelled, even after his parents had ripped up its carpeting, thrown out its bed, and emptied its closet of everything but his art, by the time I first visited them, three months after his death.*" I have no means of verifying this odor. I'm just going to have to take John's word for it.

"What I know for certain about Levi Presley, in other words, is whatever Gail, his mom, and Levi Senior . . ." The names of Levi's parents are confirmed in the Coroner's Report.

". . . his dad . . ." Technically, Levi's father's name is "Levi III," since on the Coroner's Report Levi is named "Levi IV."

"'Whatever you want,' they said. 'We'll go on the record about anything.'" I'm going to have to take him at his word on this, too. But for the record, I'm a little suspicious of this. John says that it took him "months" to get the Presleys to agree to talk with him. And yet in the essay, immediately upon meeting John, the Presleys decide to throw open their lives to this total stranger? I've never met John in person so I can't speak to his animal magnetism, but it sounds like he's tooting his look-at-me-I-have-kind-eyes-and-am-so-empathetic-that-people-just-want-to-tell-me-their-stories horn.

"There was the one that happened on a Saturday, July 13, at approximately 6:01 p.m. . . ." Temporal Inaccuracy: The rounding here of the time to "6:01 p.m." is inaccurate, since it happened at 6:01:43 p.m., which is closer to 6:02 than it is to 6:01.

". . . on the herringboned brickwork . . ." Brick pattern confirmed. The driveway is paved with bricks that are laid in 90 degree herringbones. This eventually fades into a design of overlapping arcs once you approach the entrance to the casino.

". . . of the Stratosphere Hotel and Casino's north entrance driveway . . ." The Coroner's Report confirms the directionality of this as "north." But there's a contradiction among the sources themselves. The Coroner's Report says: "The area where the decedent was found is the north asphalt driveway that leads into the main entrance of the hotel/ casino." This is confusing, because when I went to investigate the "north asphalt driveway" (as the Coroner's Report calls it) or the "north entrance driveway" (as John calls it) I found an area that was paved with brick, not asphalt. And in addition, while there is an entrance to the casino on this side of the building, it really couldn't be called the "main entrance," as there are several entrances all around the building, and each seems to be equally well-used. So in this case, oddly enough, the Coroner's Report seems to be incorrect. In addition, the entrance isn't actually called the "north entrance driveway"; the door this driveway leads to is labeled "Door 5S." And for that matter, this "driveway," while technically reserved for cars, doesn't actually seem to be accessible from the street. It looks like it's a lot for valet parking only. So can it even be called a "driveway"?

". . . a hot night . . ." The warmth of the night is confirmed by local weather records. The temperature didn't drop below 99 degrees all night, and was above 111 degrees from about two o'clock in the afternoon until well after 7:00 p.m.

". . . the winds from the east . . ." Factual Dispute: The online *Weather Underground* report for that day says that for most of the night the wind was blowing SW/S/SSW, meaning it was blowing from the northeast, not the east. I think John just misread the wind directions. It's a common mistake.

". . . blowing white palls of dust . . ." Factual Dispute: At the time of Levi's death, the wind was blowing about 11.5 mph, which on the Beaufort Scale is considered a "gentle breeze." True, the maximum wind speed for the day was 28 mph—or what is considered a "strong breeze"— and there were wind gusts of a maximum of 38 mph—which is considered "near gale" force. However, the text in question is describing the condition at 6:01 p.m., and the maximum wind speeds for the day didn't hit until around 10:00 p.m. that night. So it's unlikely that the wind was sufficient enough to blow "white palls of dust."

John: It's adding drama, Jim. Plus, I don't think it takes much wind to blow dust. I'm sure that there was a little handful of dust somewhere in the city at that time that was being kicked up by the wind. You can let it go.

But, among those who did not know Levi Presley personally, among those in Las Vegas who only knew of this boy by body or rumor or newscast or name, what officially would be placed on the record about his death, and what officially would be taken off it, and what officially, from the very start, would never be allowed to get anywhere near that record of Levi Presley's death, would come to contrast so completely the eager openness of Levi's parents that there appeared at times to exist two entirely different versions of Levi Presley's suicide. There was the one that happened on a Saturday, July 13, at approximately 6:01 p.m., on the herringboned brickwork of the Stratosphere Hotel and Casino's north entrance driveway, a hot night, the winds from the east blowing white palls of dust,

"... the stock market low, unemployment rates high ..." Confirmed: In the second to third quarter of 2002, which is when Levi Presley died, economic times were tough—the Dow Jones was at a low of about 8600. The high for that year was 10600, in March, and the lowest for the year was 7530, in October. The NASDAQ, which peaked in January at 2022, was at 1300 in mid-July when Levi died, while the S&P and NYSE were also both low for the year.

"... the moon only showing half of itself ..." Factual Dispute: The moon was showing significantly less than "half of itself." At the time during the month when Levi Presley died, the moon was in a "waxing crescent" phase, which means that only 12 percent of the moon was illuminated, according to the *Weather Underground*.

"... and Mars and Jupiter aligned ..." This "alignment" is accurate for the most part, although the terminology John's using is not really precise. Mars and Jupiter were within 9 degrees longitude of each other, according to the website *Astro.com*. This, however, according to *Astrology.com*, is considered a "conjunction," not an "alignment."

the stock market low, unemployment rates high, the moon only showing half of itself, and Mars and Jupiter aligned, which isn't particularly rare, and so there is no phenomenon to which one in desperation might try to attribute the disparity of facts that surround this particular death's most blunt fact: that Levi Presley's body had been found "supine" and "damaged" but "relatively intact" on the driveway of the Stratosphere Hotel and Casino, according to the coroner of Clark County, Nevada; or that Levi Presley's body had been found "splattered to a million pieces" on the driveway of the Stratosphere Hotel and Casino, according to a police report; or that parts of Levi Presley had been found a day later,

interval is: 794–832 days (91%). Five other interval periods between 68–74 days and 976–981 days occur. The shortest period interval involves multiple conjunction sets and the longest skipped sets. Generally, after every 21st event, the series is broken by the longer interval period (2026–2029 and 2073–2076)." Or in lay terms: It wasn't rare.

"... that Levi Presley's body had been found 'supine' and 'damaged' but 'relatively intact' on the driveway of the Stratosphere Hotel and Casino, according to the coroner of Clark County, Nevada ..." Factual Dispute: The Coroner's Report does indeed use the word "supine," but "damaged" and "intact" are from John's notes during his interview with the coroner. So it's inaccurate to attribute the "Coroner's Report" as the source for these words, which the quotation marks imply.

John: But it's more efficient to attribute all of this to the official report, so leave it.

"... or that Levi Presley's body had been found 'splattered to a million pieces' on the driveway of the Stratosphere Hotel and Casino, according to a police report ..." Again, this isn't technically accurate. This statement comes

"... which isn't particularly rare ..." Confirmed: It's not rare. In fact, celestially speaking, it's actually quite common, occurring about every two or three years. According to the website of the Geophysical Institute of the University of Alaska, "The frequency of planet-to-planet conjunctions is a function of the degree of the planets' separation, the time period under consideration, and the number of planets involved. Conjunctions can be quite unspectacular since planets can be more than 10 degrees apart while quasi-conjunctions can be less than 0.5 degree apart for many days." Also, in the "Mars-Jupiter Conjunctions" section of that website: "Conjunction pair is visible 26% of the time based on the period 1900–2078. Conjunction

from an interview John conducted with Sergeant Tirso Dominguez of the Las Vegas Metropolitan Police. It doesn't appear in the police report itself.

John: Police statement vs. police report—they're basically the same thing. And since "report" sounds more precise, I'm leaving it.

"... or that parts of Levi Presley had been found a day later, sixty feet away and across the street, according to a witness at a nearby motel." I can't find any mention of this in the local papers, nor in an extensive Google search, nor even in John's own notes. And to be honest, this seems pretty improbable, given that the Las Vegas Boulevard median is lined with bushes and trees. There's a fast-food restaurant across the street, and even if they aren't the most fastidious germophobes I'd still think they would take it upon themselves to clean up this sort of thing in the unlikely event that the proper authorities hadn't. John?

John: Once again, Jim, this is from casually interviewing people in the neighborhood around the hotel in the days after Levi's death. The neighborhood that the Stratosphere is in is called the "Naked City," and it's not a particularly pleasant place. It's icky and depressed and many of the people I spoke with were either drunk or stoned

sixty feet away and across the street, according to a witness at a nearby motel.

And then there was the death, according to some in Las Vegas, that simply did not seem to have occurred.

or both, so these claims can't at all be taken seriously. (And I, too, doubt that the city would let body parts lie around for days.) However, this claim is here to add to the hearsay surrounding Levi's death, and also to contribute to the many discrepancies I found while researching Levi's case. For example: preceding this claim are the apparent contradictions from the Coroner's Office and the police about the condition of Levi's body after he fell. So, as unreliable as this claim about "body parts" is, I include it in order to emphasize the looseness of the facts that seemed to surround Levi's death.

There's a general problem with the statistics in this section. Almost every statistic John cites is presented as a description of the city of Las Vegas. But in a lot of the source material he provided, some of these statistics refer to a variety of population groups, including the city of Las Vegas proper, Clark County, Nevada (of which Las Vegas is a part), and sometimes even the entire state of Nevada. The problem with this conflation, as one government employee explained to me, is that Clark County has three times the population of the city of Las Vegas. This, in other words, is not a trifling discrepancy. We may therefore want to specify that some of this information refers to Nevada, or to Clark County, rather than Las Vegas specifically. John, do you want to draft a clarification about this to add to the essay?

John: No. With all possible respect, you're actually really wrong about this, Jim. Clark County *is* Las Vegas. Sure, the county is made up of lots of communities other than Las Vegas, but these days when we refer to "Las Vegas" we are in fact usually talking about Clark County. As you noted, Las Vegas itself is a relatively small city, and geographically it's primarily limited to what's referred to these days as "downtown" Las Vegas— the old and rather seedy part of town that few tourists actually visit. Indeed, the vast majority of the Las Vegas Strip—the part of the city we think about when we hear the name "Las Vegas"—is not in Las Vegas but rather in Clark County. When the Flamingo Hotel opened in 1946, for example—the first hotel on the modern-day Strip—it opened in a town just south of Las Vegas called Paradise, Nevada, which is in Clark County. The hotel was built there because Bugsy Siegel wanted it to be outside the jurisdiction of the city of Las Vegas. Nevertheless, these days I doubt that we would consider the Flamingo, nor any of the dozens of hotels that surround it on the Strip, to be anywhere other than in "Las Vegas." So there's no discrepancy. This is the kind of streamlining that needs to be done, I think, in order to save readers from having to read ridiculously long-winded and clunky explanations like this.

"More people kill themselves in Las Vegas every year than in any other place in America." Confirmed: See Adam Goldman's article "The Suicide Capital of America," *Associated Press,* February 9, 2004.

"People kill themselves in Las Vegas so often, in fact, that one has a better chance of killing oneself in Vegas than of being killed there . . ." Confirmed. The most relevant figures for this time period that I found for being killed by someone in Las Vegas versus committing suicide are 169 homicides to 264 suicides. Most of the statistical information here and below, unless otherwise indicated, is from *Nevada Vital Statistics 2001–2003*, a publication of the State of Nevada.

More people kill themselves in Las Vegas every year than in any other place in America.

People kill themselves in Las Vegas so often, in fact, that one has a better chance of killing oneself in Vegas than of being killed there, despite the fact that Las Vegas is also one of the most dangerous cities in which to live, according to the FBI's *Uniform Crime Report*. In Las Vegas, more people kill themselves than die in car accidents,

". . . despite the fact that Las Vegas is also one of the most dangerous cities in which to live, according to the FBI's *Uniform Crime Report*." Factual Dispute: The *Uniform Crime Report* actually lists the entire state of Nevada as "the third most dangerous state" rather than Las Vegas as the third most dangerous "city." I think John massaged this fact in order to fit it into his argument. John, maybe clarify that this statistic is referencing the whole state, so as not to confuse readers?

John: Nobody's confused. I "massaged" this fact in order to *avoid* confusing people. The population of Las Vegas (or Clark County . . . whatever you want to call it) is currently about 1.9 million people, while the state as a whole is 2.6 million people. So Las Vegas accounts for 73 percent of the state's population. I think it's safe to say that a statistic that applies to the state as a whole is applicable to Las Vegas, especially when it comes to crime. Again, it's called "streamlining."

"In Las Vegas, more people kill themselves than die in car accidents . . ." Technically speaking, I guess this is true, since there were 264 suicides and 263 car accidents. But he's pushing it.

"... die of AIDS ..." Confirmed: 264 vs. 65.

"... die of pneumonia ..." Confirmed, sort of. Most statistics for pneumonia are combined with influenza, which makes it difficult to know for certain how many people died of pneumonia specifically. But since the combined number of deaths was 272, it's safe to say that pneumonia's portion of that number was lower than the number of suicides, at 264.

"... cirrhosis ..." Confirmed: 264 vs. 155.

"... diabetes ..." Confirmed: 264 vs. 191.

"Statistically speaking, the only things more likely to kill you in Las Vegas are heart disease ..." The State of Nevada reports that all deaths in Las Vegas from what it calls "diseases of the heart" totaled 3,054. So this is confirmed.

"... stroke ..." Stroke is a yes, at 679. Hey, we're on a roll!

"... and a few types of cancer." There's a need for some factual disambiguation here in order for this statement to make sense. "A few types of cancer" is just too ambiguous. It could either mean a few different biological forms of cancer, or related forms of cancer found in different parts of the body. The State of Nevada reports that there were a total of 2,762 deaths that year from cancer. But it also offers cancer statistics for different regions of the body: so, for example, there were 887 upper respiratory cancer deaths, and 275 lower intestinal tract cancer deaths. However, these are the only two specific categories of cancer deaths that outnumber the suicide rate—if, that is, we don't count the category for "other and unspecified cancer deaths," which accounted for 280 deaths. So the problem is that when one refers to a "type of cancer" one needs to keep in mind that, according to Cancer Research UK (the United Kingdom's leading organization dedicated to cancer research), there are over two hundred varieties of cancer that can affect sixty different organs of the body. Therefore, referring to "a few types of cancer" is incredibly vague and could mean any number of things. And, even running with this vagueness, according to the statistics from

die of AIDS, die of pneumonia, cirrhosis, or diabetes. Statistically speaking, the only things more likely to kill you in Las Vegas are heart disease, stroke, and a few types of cancer.

Otherwise, in Vegas, you're going to kill yourself.

the State of Nevada, even a generous interpretation is probably wrong, since only two "types" of cancer (aggregated by body region) were more deadly than suicide. It should be noted that those two regions alone can include lung cancer, tracheal cancer, colon cancer, bronchial cancer, rectal cancer, and anal cancer, and that isn't taking into account the distinct diagnoses of these cancers that are also possible. To give you an idea of how these can be further subdivided, the National Cancer Institute divides "brain cancer" alone into at least nine different categories, a few of which are themselves further divided into sub-subcategories, like: Brain Tumor, Adult; Brain Tumor, Brain Stem Glioma, Childhood; Brain Tumor, Cerebellar Astrocytoma, Childhood; Brain Tumor, Cerebral Astrocytoma/Malignant Glioma, Childhood; Brain Tumor, Ependymoma, Childhood; Brain Tumor, Medulloblastoma, Childhood; Brain Tumor, Supratentorial Primitive Neuroectodermal Tumors, Childhood; Brain Tumor, Visual Pathway and Hypothalamic Glioma, Childhood; and Brain Tumor, Childhood Other. In other words, John's use of the term "type" is meaningless. Given the statistics, then, it would be more safe to just say "cancer"—otherwise, given the sub- and sub-subcategories that cancer can be divided into, it would actually be most accurate to say that "no types of cancer" kill more people than suicide.

John: I really don't think that readers would be upset if they found out that I lumped Supratentorial Primitive Neuroectodermal Tumors and Childhood Medulloblastoma together under the category of "a few types of cancer." Please give me a break with this shit.

"Otherwise, in Vegas, you're going to kill yourself." Factual Dispute: There are actually a few other things that cause more deaths than suicide in Las Vegas. Kidney disease annually kills 357 people, compared to suicide's 264. And septicemia (blood poisoning) is also higher, at 333. And according to the State, "chronic lower respiratory diseases" (which I assume are things like chronic obstructive pulmonary disease, emphysema, chronic bronchitis, cystic fibrosis, etc.) account for more than twice the suicide deaths, at 735.

"**Maybe this is why, according to the** *Archives of Pediatric and Adolescent Medicine,* **Las Vegas also has the highest child abuse death rate for children under the age of four.**" Factual Dispute: The statistic is actually "four years *and* younger," so it includes four-year-olds. It's an inclusive <= 4 rather than a < 4. (*The Grit Beneath the Glitter,* p. 136.)

"**Or the highest rate of drug use among teenagers in the country.**" Factual Dispute: I emailed a government agency called the Substance Abuse and Mental Health Services Administration about this. I got a response from someone named Leah Young who said: "I asked the statistician who works on sub-state data for us about your query on Las Vegas. This is his reply: 'I don't think that statistic comes from us, and I'll tell you why. Las Vegas is in Clark County. Clark has about 1.6 million people according to the Census; Las Vegas only has about 0.5 million. In Nevada, we take a sample of 900 per year, which gives a 3-year sample of 2,700, with about 900 in ages 12–17. Now, that is for the whole State. Since Vegas is .5 million and Nevada is about 2.2 million, then Vegas gets less than one quarter of the population and thus less than one quarter of the sample, or about 675 cases for all persons, and about 225 for youth, if we combined all 3 years. But the area we estimated for the Nevada sub-state report was Clark County, which has a population over 3 times the size of Las Vegas. So it wouldn't be a good estimate for just Las Vegas.' I also checked one of the metropolitan releases we did, and Las Vegas wasn't one of the cities with the highest teenage drug rate. So, I don't think the data came from us." So, this SAMHSA agent is basically arguing against the point John made about the Clark County/Las Vegas conflation, since she says

that Clark County's figures should not be used for the city proper. Small Wrinkle: John's notes include a photocopy of page 76 from a book entitled *The Real Las Vegas: Life Beyond the Strip,* which actually does list this as a statistic. So, he does have a source for this. But again, according SAMHSA, it seems likely that the source is incorrect. So, what do we care about more: having a source that confirms John's claim (but is probably inaccurate), or changing John's claim so that it's genuinely accurate?

Maybe this is why, according to the *Archives of Pediatric and Adolescent Medicine,* Las Vegas also has the highest child abuse death rate for children under the age of four. Or the highest rate of drug use among teenagers in the country. The highest number of American arrests for driving under the influence.

The highest high school dropout rate.

Highest household bankruptcy rate.

And the highest number of divorces nationwide, every year.

According to the executive director of WestCare, the city's only full-time mental health care facility, an average of five hundred residents seek psychiatric treatment every single month in Vegas, but an estimated 49 percent of them never receive treatment. Indeed,

"**The highest number of American arrests for driving under the influence.**" Confirmed in *The Real Las Vegas: Life Beyond the Strip,* p. 85. If we still want to trust this source, that is.

"**The highest high school dropout rate.**" Confirmed in *The Grit Beneath the Glitter;* however, the statistic is from 1999.

"**Highest household bankruptcy rate.**" Confirmed by Bob Lawless in "Bankruptcy Filing Rates by District, April 2006–March 2008," at *CreditSlips.org.*

"**And the highest number of divorces nationwide, every year.**" Confirmed in *The Grit Beneath the Glitter;* but it is still a very old statistic.

"**According to the executive director of WestCare, the city's only full-time mental health care facility, an average of five hundred residents seek psychiatric treatment every single month in Vegas, but an estimated 49 percent of them never receive treatment.**" Most of this is right, according to the article "Mind Matters" by Larry Wills in the *Las Vegas Mercury,* April 29, 2004. But this estimation was made by a woman in the article named JoAnn Lujan, who is the executive director of the "triage crisis center" at WestCare, not the director of the entire organization.

"Indeed, in a nation in which an average of thirty-three hospital beds for every 100,000 patients are typically devoted to psychiatric care, Las Vegas devotes just four beds out of 100,000 to treat its mentally ill." This can be confirmed for Clark County in general. But it isn't applicable to Las Vegas specifically. Also, the statistic is 4.5 beds per 100,000, not 4 beds per 100,000 ("Five Reasons WestCare Needs To Be Saved" by Damon Hodge, *Las Vegas Weekly,* July 15, 2004).

"Some speculate . . ." John provides no sources to support the claim that anyone is speculating about this. Or perhaps he's the one who's doing the speculating. Can he count himself as the "some" he's referring to?

"According to a 2000 report in the *Las Vegas Sun,* the homeless rate in Las Vegas nearly quadrupled in the 1990s—from 2,000 people in 1989 to 18,000 people in 1999 . . ." The raw data is correct. But there's a problem with the rate estimate. If we take these numbers without question, the rate of increase from "2,000" to "18,000" for the respective population sizes at that time would be about 4.88, which is more accurately represented by the statement "nearly quintupled," not "quadrupled."

". . . an increase that motivated voters in Las Vegas to pass new 'quality of life' laws through which dozens of downtown sweeps have since been conducted, citing 'jaywalking, sidewalk obstructing, and other violations as an excuse to arrest homeless residents and clean up problem areas' . . . " Confirmed by the *Associated Press,* "Vegas Rated Nation's Meanest City," August 5, 2003.

". . . thus leading the National Coalition for the Homeless to call Las Vegas in 2003 'the meanest city in America.'" Ditto.

"Nevertheless, according to the Nevada Development Authority's *Las Vegas Perspective* of 2005, an average of 8,000 people move into the city every single month." Name of organization and publication confirmed. But the average number of newcomers into the city was actually closer to 8,500, not 8,000, according to the "Newcomer Population" chart, which indicates that in 2004 more than 102,200 people moved to Las Vegas. When divided by 12 months, the figure is an average of 8,520 people. It's an issue of some troubling math on John's part.

"It is the fastest-growing metropolitan area in America." There isn't a source for this specific assertion, but Nevada is indeed the fastest-growing state, and Las Vegas is indeed in Nevada and is the largest part of the state. But, it's also possible that other states of larger size with lower overall growth rates have sub-pockets with faster rates of growth than

---

in a nation in which an average of thirty-three hospital beds for every 100,000 patients are typically devoted to psychiatric care, Las Vegas devotes just four beds out of 100,000 to treat its mentally ill.

Some speculate that this shortage of local treatment for the mentally ill has contributed to spikes in the city's homelessness. According to a 2000 report in the *Las Vegas Sun,* the homeless rate in Las Vegas nearly quadrupled in the 1990s—from 2,000 people in 1989 to 18,000 people in 1999—an increase that motivated voters in Las Vegas to pass new "quality of life" laws through which dozens of downtown sweeps have since been conducted, citing "jaywalking, sidewalk obstructing, and other violations as an excuse to arrest homeless residents and clean up problem areas," thus leading the National Coalition for the Homeless to call Las Vegas in 2003 "the meanest city in America."

Nevertheless, according to the Nevada Development Authority's *Las Vegas Perspective* of 2005, an average of 8,000 people move into the city every single month. It is the fastest-growing

Vegas. John is at the very least stretching this fact in order to fit his argument, and I for one am shocked.

metropolitan area in America. As a result, the Las Vegas Valley's shortage of land has become so pronounced that a local paper once reported that two new acres of land in Las Vegas are developed every hour, on each of which are squeezed an average of eight three-bedroom homes.

Fortune magazine has called Las Vegas "the best place in the country to have any kind of business."

Retirement Places has said it's "the nation's most desirable retirement community."

And *Time* magazine has named Las Vegas "The New All-American City," the same year in which a study entitled "Social Stress in the United States" ranked Las Vegas among the most stressful cities in which to live.

For every five new residents who move to Las Vegas, three natives move out.

"As a result, the Las Vegas Valley's shortage of land has become so pronounced that a local paper once reported that two new acres of land in Las Vegas are developed every hour, on each of which are squeezed an average of eight three-bedroom homes." Confirmed by Hubble Smith's "Execs: Affordable Housing in Las Vegas Hinges on Planning," *Las Vegas Review-Journal,* February 13, 2003.

"*Fortune* magazine has called Las Vegas 'the best place in the country to have any kind of business.'" Confirmed in *Fortune,* 1998.

"*Retirement Places* has said it's 'the nation's most desirable retirement community.'" Factual dispute: The article appeared in 1995, not in 1994, and the proper title of the magazine is *Retirement Places Listed.*

"And *Time* magazine has named Las Vegas 'The New All-American City' . . ." Confirmed in *The Grit Beneath the Glitter,* p. 127.

". . . the same year in which a study entitled 'Social Stress in the United States' ranked Las Vegas among the most stressful cities in which to live." This study took place in 1986, almost a decade before *Time* magazine's designation of Las Vegas as "The New All-American City," which deflates the irony I think John is going for by forcing these two things to occur in the same year. (*The Grit Beneath the Glitter,* p. 136.)

"For every five new residents who move to Las Vegas, three natives move out." Factual Dispute: According to "Seekers, Drawn to Las Vegas, Find a Broken Promised Land" by Dean E. Murphy, *New York Times,* May 30, 2004: "The Nevada state demographer, Jeff Hardcastle, said some surveys estimate that for every two new arrivals in Las Vegas and surrounding Clark County, one person leaves. The latest I.R.S. data puts the ratio closer to 1.5 to 1." So neither of these ratios equals John's claim of 5:3. The latter one comes closest, at about 5:3.33. So I guess if we're OK with dropping that fractional one-third of a person, then it jives. But John, this would be an easy fix if you wanted to rephrase it.

John: Maybe I'm being picky here, but I don't think "For every five new residents who move to Las Vegas, three and one-third residents move out" has the same syntactical resonance.

"I started to volunteer at the Las Vegas Suicide Prevention Center after moving to the city to help my mom out. The center made me sign a 'waiver of intent,' make a cash donation of $100, and take a three-week-long course about the city's suicide problems." John has this 'waiver of intent' in his notes, which states that volunteers can't discuss with the press what went on at the hotline (which, by the way, he seems to be violating). But I can't find any receipt for this donation. I also can't find any confirmation of this move he made to Vegas to "help [his] mother out." John, any receipts from movers and the Suicide Prevention Center that you could fax me? Also, is there any way I could get your mom's phone number to confirm the timing of all this?

John: I'm not in the habit of asking for receipts for donations. You're also getting nowhere near my mom.

"'Some people say it's drugs, and others say it's stress, and of course there are always people who blame our suicides on the gambling,' explained Marjorie Westin, the director of the center." The basic gist of this quote is in John's notes, although not in this exact order syntactically. Plus, he changed this woman's name; her real name is Dorothy Bryant. Also, just FYI: in the *Suicide Prevention Center of Clark County Administrative Policy and Procedures* packet (more on that later) there is a section that says "statements or stories to news media or for publication will be made only by authorized staff with aproval from the Director. No statements or stories should mention the prevention center or its services without this specific authorization." In the margins John has written, apparently rhetorically, "Could I just change everyone's name, including the organization's name?" So I guess he made up his mind about that . . .

"There are twenty-three people who volunteer for the center . . ." Factual Dispute: According to an article in the *Las Vegas Mercury*, there are thirty people who volunteer for the Las Vegas hotline, although the article was published two years after John was a volunteer, so perhaps the hotline has since added volunteers ("Lives on the Line" by Andrew Kiraly, *Las Vegas Mercury*, December 16, 2004).

". . . one of whom is on duty at any given time, receiving calls in his or her own private home." Confirmed in "Calling for Help" by Joan Whitley, *Las Vegas Review-Journal*, March 9, 2000.

"This is a variation on the standard hotline system in which two trained counselors usually answer calls together, providing each other support in a centralized location." Confirmed by Stacy Willis in "Stopping Suicide: Nevada Lags Behind Nation in Prevention Programs," *Las Vegas Sun*, November 23, 2001.

I started to volunteer at the Las Vegas Suicide Prevention Center after moving to the city to help my mom out. The center made me sign a "waiver of intent," make a cash donation of $100, and take a three-week-long course about the city's suicide problems.

"Some people say it's drugs, and others say it's stress, and of course there are always people who blame our suicides on the gambling," explained Marjorie Westin, the director of the center. "But I've been studying this city's problem for my entire adult life, and none of those theories are right. The truth is that nobody wants to hear the real answer about suicide."

Marjorie Westin founded the Las Vegas Suicide Prevention Center when she was still a graduate student, thirty-five years ago. There are twenty-three people who volunteer for the center, one of whom is on duty at any given time, receiving calls in his or her own private home. This is a variation on the standard hotline system in which two

". . . the Las Vegas Suicide Prevention Center employs a local answering service to screen its hotline calls . . ." Ditto.

"Sometimes, however, the American Telephone Answering Service itself gets overloaded. Sometimes it asks callers to leave messages for the center. Sometimes refers callers to hotlines out of state. Sometimes doesn't even manage to answer calls at all. According to a study by the *Las Vegas Sun* in 2001, in fact, only 55 percent of the paper's calls ever reached a hotline counselor." Technically, the raw figures here are correct. But the paper didn't so much do a scientific "study" as an informal test. They called the hotline 20 times and were connected to a counselor 11 times out of those 20, which is 55 percent. The article also states that "one call went unanswered, two calls received fax tones and six calls went to an answering service . . . [and] of those that went to the answering service, five were referred to another organization's out-of-town suicide hotline, and one caller was asked to leave a message" ("Stopping Suicide: Nevada Lags Behind Nation in Prevention Programs" by Stacy J. Willis, *Las Vegas Sun,* November 23, 2001). An article in the *Review-Journal* states: "Sometimes the Las Vegas center, which advertises itself as a 24-hour service, has no one to answer the hotline. During those unfilled shifts—which account for about 18 hours a week, according to the director—its answering service refers callers to the statewide suicide prevention line run by the Reno center" ("Suicide-Prevention Experts Say More Needs to be Done to Reach Vulnerable People" by Joan Whitely, *Las Vegas Review-Journal,* March 9, 2000). However, while both articles say that sometimes calls are forwarded to out-of-town suicide numbers, nowhere in these articles is a reference made to "toll numbers out of state."

trained counselors usually answer calls together, providing each other support in a centralized location.

But given the volume of calls that the Vegas center receives, plus the dearth of volunteers who are available to work, the Las Vegas Suicide Prevention Center employs a local answering service to screen its hotline calls, which then forwards the "important" ones to a volunteer on duty.

Sometimes, however, the American Telephone Answering Service itself gets overloaded. Sometimes it asks callers to leave messages for the center. Sometimes refers callers to hotlines out of state. Sometimes doesn't even manage to answer calls at all. According to a study by the *Las Vegas Sun* in 2001, in fact, only 55 percent of the paper's calls ever reached a hotline counselor.

On my first day of class at the Suicide Prevention Center, I drove east down Flamingo Road in search of the hotline's office, miles away from the Las Vegas Strip, beneath the many overpasses leading out of town.

For a few more dusty miles I drove south on Sandhill Road, a street so removed from what most visitors ever

"I drove east down Flamingo Road in search of the hotline's office, miles away from the Las Vegas Strip, beneath the many overpasses leading out of town." According to Google maps, the trip down Flamingo Road is indeed east of the Las Vegas Strip. But, depending on where John was coming from or where he was living, it's unclear if he would have actually traveled east on this road to get there. In any case, if he's coming from the Strip, the route down Flamingo Road to Sandhill Road wouldn't intersect with any major interstate, even though he claims it does. But he's correct in his claim that it is "miles away" from the Strip—exactly 4.4 miles.

"For a few more dusty miles I drove south on Sandhill Road, a street so removed from what most visitors ever see . . ." The document I have confirming the center's location says that it's at 3342 South Sandhill Road. But again according to Google maps, that's only a mile off Flamingo Road, and you'd have to travel north to get there, not south.

"...that a woman at a bus stop..." No record of this exchange is in John's notes. I guess if he doesn't take notes during interviews he probably doesn't take notes while driving either.

"On the way to the hotline center are nursing homes ... and in an otherwise empty parking lot there is a small idle fleet of purple dog-grooming vans." Factual Nudging: The actual names of most of these businesses have been altered by John from the following: "The Helene Gregory Talent Center," "Tweety Nails," and "Rapid Medical Supplies, Inc." Also, John's notes describe pink dog-grooming vans rather than purple ones. According to local listings, Mugshots Lounge is located at 1120 North Boulder Highway in Henderson, Nevada, which is 7 miles from this location. Omelet House is at 316 North Boulder Highway in Las Vegas (also not near this location). And Al Phillips the Cleaner is on East Desert Inn Road. The big shocker is that Rapid Medical Supplies and 24-Hour Real Estate are indeed at the intersection that I think John is referring to.

John: I needed the two beats in "purple," so I changed the color. Again, I don't think it's that big a deal.

Jim: And the other changes?

"...an alcohol-free bar called Easy Does It..." The name "Easy Does It" and the quote are in John's notes, although I can't find a listing for the bar in any local directory to confirm its location.

see that a woman at a bus stop from whom I asked directions shook her head and looked again at my out-of-state license plate.

"No," she said, turning her head away. "Can't help you."

On the way to the hotline center are nursing homes and trailer parks and the low-rise pink motels that offer rentals by the month. There is Omelet House and Mugshots Lounge and Al Phillips' Cleaners—FLAGS CLEANED FOR FREE. There is an intersection with Desert Inn Road where six different strip malls anchor the roads' four corners. There is 24-Hour Real Estate—NOW OPEN 24 HRS!—The Helene Talent Agency—FREE TALENT CONSOLATIONS—and Jane's Attractive Birds—BUY ONE GET TWO FREE. There is Famous Nails, Rapid Medical, and in an otherwise empty parking lot there is a small idle fleet of purple dog-grooming vans.

Sharing a block with the Suicide Prevention Center is an alcohol-free bar called Easy Does It—THE DOORS THAT GOD OPENS NO MAN CAN CLOSE—a card shop that offers HIV testing, and a bike rack with an empty chain padlocked to nothing.

The center itself, it turned out on my arrival, is an unmarked building of one-

"...a card shop that offers HIV testing..." John's notes indicate a card shop. But nothing about HIV testing. John doesn't have a name for this card shop in his notes either, so it's hard to confirm that it's where he claims it is.

"...a bike rack with an empty chain padlocked to nothing." Nothing in his notes about this. But it seems unlikely that in such a car-centric town as Las Vegas there would be a bike rack in front of a random strip mall way off the Strip. I have a hard enough time finding bike racks where I live, and it's bike-hipster central over here.

"The center itself, it turned out on my arrival, is an unmarked building of one-room offices—a consortium of temp agencies, telemarketers, personal-injury lawyers, and an organization that calls itself Backyards of America, Inc. ..." In John's notes, the office is described as being in a small stucco house; the other details John offers about this structure are absent. However, there is a "Backyards of America" that's listed in the local business pages in Las Vegas, so that's something.

"'. . . there are three hundred suicides in the city of Las Vegas. That's one suicide every twenty-six hours. So if I've got twenty-three volunteers taking six-hour shifts, well . . . you do the math. This is a losing battle.'" This number is inflated, according to the State of Nevada's own estimate of 264 suicides in Las Vegas annually. That works out to be about one suicide every 33 hours. (Which, while slightly better than the director's claim, is still staggering.) But even within the director's own statement the math is incorrect, because if there were 300 suicides a year, then the rate would be one every 29 hours.

"In comparison, the Suicide Crisis Call Line in Reno upstate is a twenty-four-hour center with a rotating staff of sixty-five volunteers, each of whom receives fifty-six hours of professional training, and all of whom are certified by the American Association of Suicidology." Such a thing as the American Association of Suicidology does indeed exist. And the Reno group's website (which is actually called the "Crisis Call Center") confirms that it is accredited by this organization, although the website suggests that it's the organization as a whole that is certified rather than individual members. I guess that's acceptable. But the group's website also says that they have seventy trained volunteers, not sixty-five. And instead of being trained for 56 hours, the site says that "Crisis Line and Sexual Assault Support Services volunteers receive 60+ hours of intensive training over a six-week period." However, there is a Las Vegas Review-Journal article in John's notes that gives the figures of sixty-five volunteers and fifty-six hours. So, not sure what to do here. Again, this seems to be a case of John not so much making stuff up as simply using a source that contradicts facts from another source.

"'But their hotline is in a city of 400,000 people, and every year their budget is $100,000. Las Vegas has a population almost five times that size, and a suicide rate that's six times higher. The most I ever get in funding is $15,000.'" These population numbers seem to be the result of creative math on someone's part. According to the 2000 U.S. Census Bureau, Reno has 180,000 people, but the number I think John is riffing off is a figure for all of Washoe County, which has 339,486 people. Alternately, according to the same Census, Las Vegas has a population of 478,434, while all of

room offices—a consortium of temp agencies, telemarketers, personal-injury lawyers, and an organization that calls itself Backyards of America, Inc.—all of which share a single bathroom, a single secretary, and a conference table in the middle of the building's one hallway.

"I wish we had the luxury of an actual phone bank," said Marjorie. "And if we had the right funding and enough volunteers, of course I would prefer that we have a whole team of people here. But every year, without fail, there are three hundred suicides in the city of Las Vegas. That's one suicide every twenty-six hours. So if I've got twenty-three volunteers taking six-hour shifts, well . . . you do the math. This is a losing battle."

In comparison, the Suicide Crisis Call Line in Reno upstate is a twenty-four-hour center with a rotating staff of sixty-five volunteers, each of whom receives fifty-six hours of professional training, and all of whom are certified by the American Association of Suicidology.

"Some people assume the Reno center is better than ours," said Marjorie. "But their hotline is in a city of 400,000 people, and every year their budget is

Clark County has 1,375,765 people. But even if we were to go with the improper use of these population figures, 1.3 million people is nowhere near "five times" the population of Reno. Even the most recent population estimates for Las Vegas and Clark County (as opposed to the populations around the time Levi died) are 570,000 and 1,710,551, respectively. So these figures are a mess no matter how they're sliced. In terms of money given to the Las Vegas center, a *Las Vegas Sun* article from 2001 confirms that $100,000 was granted to the Reno center by the state, but the group's website says they have an annual budget of $1 million (as they put it, "Funding sources include individual donations, government, corporate and foundation grants, United Way and fee-for-service contracts . . ."). The Vegas hotline was given $10,000 by Clark County and $5,000 by Las Vegas—although I doubt that that's really a maximum figure for how much they ever get, especially if they are receiving donations from other sources, such as John's alleged donation. I guess it depends on how you interpret what is implied behind "funding," and whether that includes only public monies or whether private donations should count too.

$100,000. Las Vegas has a population almost five times that size, and a suicide rate that's six times higher. The most I ever get in funding is $15,000. Reno's hotline isn't better. Reno is what's better. Theirs is a city that cares."

During my training with two other volunteers, I learned about what Marjorie called "the perfect hotline call."

"The best call," she said, "will result in five answers to these five basic questions: First of all, who are they? Obviously, the reason you want to know who a caller is is so that you can use their name in conversation to make them feel more comfortable. Then, what are they planning on doing? Do they just want to chat, or do they have a gun in their hand? Then, where are they? Are they home, in their car, in a public place? We have a lot of hotels in Las Vegas, right? So 'How to Handle Calls from the Major Hotels' is the chapter in our manual that will help you with that one. Now, when are they going to do this? There's a difference, of course, between someone who's having a bad day, and someone who's just swallowed a whole bottle of Seconal. And so that brings us to 'how.' We've talked about guns and we've talked about pills,

" ' . . . the perfect hotline call.' [etc.]" Parts of this conversation and the quotes leading up to when he starts receiving calls are in his notes, but not everything is. I also can't find this "manual" anywhere in the box of material John sent us. John, do you have an actual "manual" you could send me?

John: I gave you everything I had.

" 'So "How to Handle Calls from the Major Hotels" is the chapter in our manual . . .' " Again, I don't know what John means by "manual" here. This information looks like it's coming from one loose sheet of paper in a three-ring binder. This could hardly be considered a "chapter" from a "manual." It's also in a completely different font from the rest of the packet.

John: Yeah, so? It was a rinky-dink operation, Jim. What are you trying to suggest?

" '. . . Seconal.' " According to the National Institutes of Health, Seconal is a brand name for secobarbital, and "is used on a short-term basis to treat insomnia (difficulty falling asleep or staying asleep). It is also used to relieve anxiety before surgery. Secobarbital is in a class of medications called barbiturates. It works by slowing activity in the brain."

but of course there are many ways that we can kill ourselves. There's suffocation, there's cutting, there's hanging, immolation . . ."

"What about 'why'?" I asked during class.

"No," Marjorie said. "We don't ever ask 'why.'"

"Why not?" I asked.

"Because 'why' is what gets asked in therapy with a counselor. It's not something we can handle on our hotline, hon. What we offer is information, like where to find a therapist so they can get themselves some help. Asking 'why' will open up a whole big can of worms. Trust me, it gets messy. You don't want to deal with 'why.'"

"Why do you feel like the world is going to come to an end?" I later asked a caller my first night of volunteering.

"Because it isn't going to come to a beginning."

I was home, at my mom's, taking the calls that the answering service forwarded to my cell.

We had the television on.

The cat was on her back.

My mom was beading jewelry to make some extra cash.

One man called to masturbate while he whispered "I'm so lonely."

A lot of people hung up after silence or just breathing.

One woman called while crying during the local evening news, screaming at me, "Whore!" when the weather forecast started.

"My mom was beading jewelry to make some extra cash." Since he won't give me his mother's contact information, I can't confirm this, nor whether or not she really has a cat, and a need for "some extra cash." Though she must be quite the artist to be able to sell her handicrafts for extra cash.

John: Tread very carefully, asshole.

"One man called to masturbate while he whispered 'I'm so lonely.'" I can kind of confirm these calls in John's "Suicide Prevention Log." It's only one-page long, however, and it details just three calls for that night—one from a guy who "jerked off while talking to me" (as John notes), another who hung up on him, and one

from the woman he mentions below. But by the way: gross.

"A lot of people hung up after silence or just breathing." Confirmed.

"One woman called while crying during the local evening news, screaming at me, 'Whore!' when the weather forecast started." This call is documented somewhat. But not in the kind of detail John offers here. His notes mention a call happening at 6:53 p.m. (presumably around the time of the local evening news). The passage states: "Woman called, very upset + hard to understand, explained that she (thought she) was a whore, was raped." The rest seems to have been fleshed out by John's imagination.

I sat that night with the manual on my lap for six hours, sometimes opened up to the chapter DO'S AND DON'TS—"Don't ever dare a caller to 'go ahead and do it'"—and sometimes to the chapter on SUICIDE FACTS AND FABLES—"Suicide is believed to be contagious among teens"—and sometimes to the chapter on USEFUL INFORMA-TION—"If somebody's calling you, they probably want your help"—but I could never figure out which information I should use, how much talking I should do, how much listening, be how friendly, exactly how much to feel.

What I realized quickly on the hotline that summer is that I do not know how to fix a problem if that problem is someone's solution.

People would call the hotline and I would start to understand. Instead of saying "no," "you're overreacting," "everything will be fine," I would sit sometimes and nod, forgetting that there were answers I was supposed to have to give.

Yet as each new caller reached the line, instinctively I reached out for the

"I sat that night with the manual on my lap for six hours, sometimes opened up to the chapter DO'S AND DON'TS—'Don't ever dare a caller to "go ahead and do it" ' . . ." Factual Dispute: So again, it has to be stated for the record that these aren't so much "chapters" as they are single sheets of paper that look more like memos, and they're collected together in a binder with titles like "Suicide Prevention Center Do's and Don'ts" and "Be Aware of Do's and Don'ts." (I'm not the copyeditor, but I think it really should be "Dos and Don'ts"—that's what the *New York Times* uses in any case.) At any rate, the origin of this first quote from the "manual" is actually in the second of those sheets, "Be Aware," not "Do's and Don'ts."

John: I'm calling it a "manual" because that's what the hotline called it. And I'm calling these "chapters" because "chapter" works better than "single sheet of paper." I'm not going to say "sometimes opened up to the single sheet of paper entitled DO'S AND DON'TS . . ."

". . . sometimes to the chapter on SUICIDE FACTS AND FABLES—'Suicide is believed to be contagious among teens' . . ." This is confirmed on the "Facts and Fables" sheet.

". . . sometimes to the chapter on USEFUL INFORMATION—'If somebody's calling you, they probably want your help' . . ." This one isn't in the "manual" at all. It actually comes from John's notes during class. It looks like it's a quote from "Marjorie," the hotline director.

"People would call the hotline and I would start to understand. Instead of saying 'no,' 'you're overreacting,' 'everything will be fine,' I would sit sometimes and nod, forgetting that there were answers I was supposed to have to give." His log doesn't cover things he said to people, just things people said to him. So, I can't confirm this.

"Yet as each new caller reached the line, instinctively I reached out for the hotline's bulky manual, its lists of things to do, a bag of Swedish Fish, my mother for a stick with an orange feather on it, and my mother's cat, with just her eyes, for some movement in the air." I think that harping on this issue of the "manual" is going to be futile, but I still will note for the record that this document is not particularly bulky. "Swedish Fish" is spelled correctly (checked the website). And I'm not going to try to confirm whether or not his mom has a cat, because I suspect that even if I asked for its name John would get offended again.

"It was Saturday . . ." Since the piece seems to imply that the person who called John was Levi Presley and that he did so on the day Presley died, I can confirm that indeed this was a Saturday, as detailed in section One.

". . . and hot . . ." Ditto, section One.

". . . the wind was blowing hard but did not come in the house." I've already established this to be imprecise, as there was no heavy wind that evening at the time of Levi Presley's death, which is when John was supposedly working on the hotline.

"Only half of it arrived." Also established earlier to be false. Only 12 percent of the moon was visible that night.

"A young boy called briefly . . ." While John made notes in his journal about the calls from the masturba-

tor and the "whore," he made no such notes about this young boy whom he implies is/would later assume was Levi. Since this is important: John?

John: I don't see the problem. I am noting right there in the text that at the time of this boy's call I didn't make much of it. It didn't strike me as significant until after I learned of Levi's death that night. There'd be no need to write about it in my journal; there was nothing about the call that was important.

Jim: But, you made notes of calls from masturbators, heavy breathers, and the self-identified "whore," so why not of this call too, especially since it looks like there weren't many calls that night—at least according to your notes. In other words, it seems like you couldn't have been too busy to jot down a note about this kid calling. Plus, as I flip ahead in this piece, I see that in section Seven you're actually quoting verbatim from this call with the boy, despite the fact that it "wasn't significant" and you didn't write down anything about your exchange.

John: It's called memory, Jim. And your accusation is inappropriate.

Jim: I'm just doing my job. I've been asked to be very thorough, John, please understand that. And OK, I'll take your point. We'll call it "memory."

"And then my shift continued on through *Hitler and the Occult* and *Trading Spaces: Boston* . . ." Surprisingly, this Hitler program actually exists, and it's described

hotline's bulky manual, its lists of things to do, a bag of Swedish Fish, my mother for a stick with an orange feather on it, and my mother's cat, with just her eyes, for some movement in the air.

It was Saturday and hot and the wind was blowing hard but did not come in the house.

The moon began to show up. Only half of it arrived.

A young boy called briefly, didn't say very much.

And then my shift continued on through *Hitler and the Occult* and *Trad-*

in detail on the homepage of one Jerry Craw, a retired systems analyst and computer programmer who apparently has a large database of the summaries of his 4,512 videotapes of TV shows, "with over 13,414 titles . . . available for checkout by family and friends." The broadcast of *Trading Spaces: Boston* is also confirmed.

"**. . . the local late-night news, on which a white and mottled sheet was shown rumpled on the ground. Blue lights. Someone's shoes. The red pavilion entry of the Stratosphere Hotel, around which a perimeter with yellow tape was drawn.**" There are no notes provided for this, which once again is rather surprising given the significance that John is trying to inject into it. Neither could I find any reference or support for this "red pavilion entry" at the Stratosphere Hotel. Source?

John: It's brick, therefore: red. And the area surrounding the entrance is a wide expanse of empty paved space, so I'm calling it a pavilion.

Jim: OK. Fair enough, I guess, if you want to invent an official-sounding name for it. But when I went to the Stratosphere there was nothing "red" about this entrance. The driveway, as I've noted earlier, was just brick. And the brick I saw was brown.

ing Spaces: Boston **and the local late-night news, on which a white and mottled sheet was shown rumpled on the ground. Blue lights. Someone's shoes. The red pavilion entry of the Stratosphere Hotel, around which a perimeter with yellow tape was drawn.**

4

The goal of the statistics in this section seems to be not so much to make a series of factually true statements, but rather to show that there are a lot of inconsistent statements made about suicide. Therefore, in this section I mostly looked for evidence that the things in John's statements were at least asserted by someone—somewhere, at some point in time—rather than trying to verify the truth of what's asserted. Not unreasonably, I did not attempt to cross-check every study done on suicide risk factors, nor even on the reliability of the studies I did consult. In other words, I'll try to restrain myself and will give John some leeway here.

"It's estimated that only 40 percent of suicides are the result of chemical imbalance. The remaining 60 percent are caused by 'undetermined factors.'" No source for this, and I couldn't find anything that says this. Most likely, "It's estimated [by John] that . . ."

"We know that people . . ." First of all, there's a problem with the generality of the term "people." Is it meant to include everyone in the world, across all cultures, or just Americans? Or does it consider people only in the developed world where these kinds of studies are done and where more rigorous statistics are usually kept? Also, almost all of the studies I've looked at so far seem to be limited to specific geographic, socioeconomic, or cultural groups, so this statement is too vague to have any merit.

". . . four times more likely to kill themselves in a city than any other kind of environment." "Confirmed": "Differences Between Urban and Rural Suicides" by E. Isometsa et al., in *Acta Psychiatrica* 95(1997): 297–305. However, this journal is from Finland, so I'm not sure how relevant it is to the point John is trying to make.

"We also know, however, that rural can be bad." Also Confirmed: "Suicide Numbers Up in Rural Iowa," *Daily Iowan*, June 11, 2010.

It's estimated that only 40 percent of suicides are the result of chemical imbalance. The remaining 60 percent are caused by "undetermined factors."

We know that people are four times more likely to kill themselves in a city than any other kind of environment.

We also know, however, that rural can be bad.

As are the hours between noon and six.

Or May.

Or winter.

"As are the hours between noon and six." Source Discrepancy: I've found one report that suggests that the hours 8:00–11:00 a.m. are particularly dangerous for ages 45 and up, while the hours 4:00–7:00 p.m. are dangerous for younger people ("Diurnal Variations in Suicide by Age and Gender in Italy" by A. Preti and P. Miotto, *Journal of Affective Disorders* 65, no. 3 [August 2001]: 253–61). Another article states, however, that "suicide attempts were more frequent between the hours of 6:00–9:00 p.m. in males and 3:00–6:00 p.m. in females" ("Climatic and Diurnal Variation in Suicide Attempts in the ED," *American Journal of Emergency Medicine* 21, no. 4 (July 2003): 271). So it seems that there's no real consensus on this issue.

"Or May." Confirmed: One study says that "a significant seasonal variation was detected in suicide attempts with a markedly bi-seasonal pattern amongst females with peaks in May and October; only a cyclic pattern was observed for males with a peak in summer" ("A Comparison of Seasonal Variation between Suicide Deaths and Attempts in Hong Kong SAR," *Journal of Affective Disorders* 81, no. 3 [September 2004]: 251–57.) A number of other studies also indicate peaks in spring.

"Or winter." Confirmed: Seasonal Affective Disorder and its side effects have been frequently documented, for example in "Seasonal Affective Disorders" by S. Atezaz Saeed and Timothy J. Bruce, *American Family Physician,* March 15, 1998. But another article ("Seasonal Variation of Suicides and Homicides in Finland: With Special Attention to Statistical Techniques Used in Seasonality Studies" by Helinä Hakko) asserts that it is generally well-documented that spring and summer see the highest incidents of suicide, while winter sees the lowest, and that "factors that trigger summer and winter depression might also be risk factors for suicide. However, studies that have actually investigated either the prevalence of SAD among suicide victims or the incidence of suicides among patients with SAD are lacking. In a follow-up study of patients diagnosed as suffering from SAD, only one patient out of 124 was identified [as having] committed [suicide] (Thompson et al. 1995)." However, since a few studies do mention winter, we could let this stand, since all he's trying to suggest here is that some researchers asserted this. Fine.

"Or if you don't drink coffee your chances of suicide are three times higher than if you did." Confirmed: "A Prospective Study of Coffee Drinking and Suicide in Women," *Archives of Internal Medicine* 156, no. 5 (March 11, 1996): 521–25.

"Ditto if you are a woman who uses the pill instead of a diaphragm . . ." Confirmed: One study I found specifically stated that the hormonal aspects of birth control pills can lead to suicide. Presumably the diaphragm does not have the same effect ("Do the Emotional Side Effects of Hormonal Contraceptives Come from Pharmacologic or Psychological Mechanisms?" *Medical Hypotheses* 63, no. 2 [2004]: 268–73).

". . . are a man with tattoos on his neck or lower arms . . ." There was a study conducted on the relationship between tattoo occurrence in young males and the prevalence of suicide that cites tattoos as a possible risk factor, explaining that "tattoos may be possible markers for lethality from both suicide and accidental death in young people, presumably because of shared risk factors such as substance abuse and personality disorder," but that "the clinical value of inquiring about tattoos in young people at risk of suicide needs further study" ("A Case-Control Study of Tattoos in

Young Suicide Victims as a Possible Marker of Risk," *Journal of Affective Disorders* 59, no. 2 [August 2000]: 165–68).

". . . are a child with green eyes . . ." This seems too ludicrous to investigate.

". . . have any silver fillings." Confirmed: Apparently fillings can add to suicide risk if they have mercury in them, as depression leading to suicide is consistent with a diagnosis of mercury toxicity ("The Dental Amalgam Issue" by DAMS Inc., August 2005).

Or if you don't drink coffee your chances of suicide are three times higher than if you did.

Ditto if you are a woman who uses the pill instead of a diaphragm, are a man with tattoos on his neck or lower arms, are a child with green eyes, have any silver fillings.

If you were born under the signs of Aries, Gemini, or Leo: that is bad.

You are more likely to want to kill yourself during a new moon than a full one. More if you don't have pets, more

"If you were born under the signs of Aries, Gemini, or Leo: that is bad." I couldn't find anything remotely close to confirming this, which makes sense, because I seriously doubt that any reputable clinicians would try to find astrological patterns in suicide. John probably made this up.

"You are more likely to want to kill yourself during a new moon than a full one." Amazingly enough, the abstract of a study on "Lunar Association with Suicide" says that—at least among participants in Cuyahoga County, Ohio, for 1972–75—when you look at suicides by year, month, day of week, lunar phase, and holiday occurrence, "only lunar phase demonstrates a significant variation in suicide rate; an increase is observed in this sample with respect to new moon phase but not for full moon phase" ("Lunar Association with Suicide," *Suicide and Life Threatening Behavior* 7, no. 1 [Spring 1977]: 31–39).

"More if you don't have pets . . ." Confirmed: A Florida Mental Health Institute guide entitled "Youth Suicide Prevention" says that "responsibility for pets"

decreases suicide risks, so I suppose the inverse should apply.

if you own a gun, more if you earn between $32,000 and $58,000 a year.

More if you're male.

More if you're white.

More if you're over sixty-five.

It helps if you live anywhere in the United States other than Nevada, Wyoming, Alaska, or Montana, although the experts so far can't figure out why.

Nor have they figured out why Native Americans once tended to kill themselves more often than any other group, but then, fifteen years ago, stopped killing themselves significantly.

They do not know why, generally speaking, white suicide victims tend to

". . . more if you own a gun . . ." Confirmed. This is verbatim: "Where there are more guns, there are more suicides, the National Research Council (NRC) concluded in a report on firearm policy released last winter. Areas with higher household gun ownership rates have higher suicide rates, even when controlling for things also associated with suicide, like divorce rates and unemployment. In 2002, 31,655 Americans took their lives, 17,108 of them with firearms. Gun prevalence is not the only predictor of suicide rates. Cultural factors also play a key role. China, for example, has fewer guns and higher suicide rates than the U.S. But within the United States, the link, the National Research Council concluded, is clear" ("Fatal Connection: The Link Between Guns and Suicide" by Catherine W. Barber, *Harvard Injury Control Research Center,* September 26, 2005).

". . . more if you earn between $32,000 and $58,000 a year." Factual Dispute: Studies consistently show that in both urban and rural areas, there is a generally higher prevalence in the lowest-income groups, rather than the middle class ("Socio-Economic Inequalities in Suicide: A European Comparative Study," *British Journal of Psychiatry* 2005, 187, pp. 49–54).

"More if you're male." Confirmed: "Men and Suicide," *Men's Health,* January 4, 2007.

"More if you're white." Confirmed: "Black-White Paradox in Suicide," *Social Science and Medicine* 63, no. 8 (October 2006): 2165–75.

"More if you're over sixty-five." Confirmed: "Suicide Among the Elderly: A Fact Sheet," National Strategy for Suicide Prevention, U.S. Department of Health and Human Services, 2008.

"It helps if you live anywhere in the United States other than Nevada, Wyoming, Alaska, or Montana . . ." Confirmed by the American Association of Suicidology on their website, "Rate, Number, and Ranking of Suicide for Each U.S. State, 2003."

"Nor have they figured out why Native Americans once tended to kill themselves more often than any other group, but then, fifteen years ago, stopped killing themselves significantly." Factual Dispute: According to Nevada state statistics, there has been a general decrease in suicide among Native Americans over the last fifteen years, but I see no evidence of a "significant" drop-off occurring fifteen years ago. There have been extremely high years (1990), and very low years (2000), but it has been more erratic than anything else. According to the CDC, the "Crude Death Rate" from "Intentional Self-Harm (Suicide)" was aberrantly high in 1990 among Native Americans, but other than that the rates have fluctuated up and down. It should be noted as well that suicides among Native Americans are almost always higher than suicides among other minorities, as they are generally still quite higher than nearly everyone. According to CDC statistics in 2003, the current suicide rates for Native Americans haven't changed significantly since 1989. Between 1989 and 1998, firearm-related death rates increased 13 percent, and homicide increased 20 percent, but suicide rates remained unchanged. So I'm not sure where John's getting his information for this, nor what he's trying to suggest with it.

"They do not know why, generally speaking, white suicide victims tend to shoot themselves, while black suicide victims tend to poison themselves, Hispanics tend to hang themselves..." Factual and Linguistic Dispute: According to the data, in fact all ethnic groups "tended to" shoot themselves, in that every ethnic group killed themselves with firearms more than any other method. Granted, a higher percentage of African-Americans killed themselves by poisoning than any other group (42 percent, vs. 22 percent average), and a higher percentage of Hispanics killed themselves by hanging than any other group (32 percent vs. 14 percent average). But each group still technically "tended to" shoot themselves (as in more than 50 percent of those who committed suicide used firearms). Once again, it seems John's trying to stir up some drama here where there simply isn't any. What he could say is that these groups "disproportionately tended to" and that would be true, though still a bit misleading. (*Nevada Vital Statistics,* 2001–2003, p. 322.)

"... and teens to cut themselves." Factual Dispute: I couldn't get statistics on "teenagers" specifically, just for kids aged "5–14" and "15–24." Regardless, zero out of forty-three people ages 5–24 in the year 2000 killed themselves by "Cutting/Stabbing" (*Nevada Vital Stats* 2000, p. 125). And the stats for 2001 were 1/37 and 0/40 for 2002 for the whole state of Nevada (*Nevada Vital Statistics,* 2001–2003, pp. 323–24). So this is a complete fabrication.

"... Dr. John Fildes of the University of Nevada's College of Medicine ..." Name and position confirmed ("How Cadavers Help Save Lives" by Joseph Allen, *Las Vegas Mercury,* October 23, 2003).

"... received $1.5 million from the federal government in order to study the issue of suicide in Las Vegas ..." Confirmed: Grant is mentioned in the *American Foundation for Suicide Prevention Newsletter,* June 2001. Confirmation of the grant amount in "Grim Reaping: Suicide Prevention Center Is on Life Support" by Damon Hodge, *Las Vegas Weekly,* August 29, 2002.

"By the time I finally met Dr. Fildes in person, however, our appointment had been rescheduled four times in eight months, his federal grant had long expired, and the most that he'd concluded about the suicides of Las Vegas is that he still did not know what caused them." Nowhere in John's notes.

"It was to Sergeant Tirso Dominguez, therefore, an officer at the Las Vegas Metropolitan Police Department's Office of Public Information, that I turned for information about Las Vegas suicides. But 'I don't have a comment about anything like that,' is how Sergeant Dominguez responded to my request for information." Sergeant Dominguez's name and rank are confirmed in the *Las Vegas Weekly* article "Still Homeless for the Holidays" by Damon Hodge, December 6, 2001. And there is evidence of John having spoken to Dominguez in his notes. However, the closest I can find to this quote is the following: "I just don't want to be a part of a story about a kid who jumped off the Strato-sphere." Same general idea, but John is still playing around with the guy's words. I think it's clear (upon reading below in the piece) that John's trying to use the "no comment" line to play off what the CDC has to say about that. In other words, he's manipulating what this guy actually said in order to create a literary effect, which apparently is allowed among the writers of John's non-journalistic literary genre—for which he apparently writes all the rules.

---

shoot themselves, while black suicide victims tend to poison themselves, Hispanics tend to hang themselves, and teens to cut themselves.

Recently, Dr. John Fildes of the University of Nevada's College of Medicine received $1.5 million from the federal government in order to study the issue of suicide in Las Vegas, which is why, after the death of Levi Presley at the Stratosphere Hotel, his office was the first I called for information about local suicides.

By the time I finally met Dr. Fildes in person, however, our appointment had been rescheduled four times in eight months, his federal grant had long expired, and the most that he'd concluded about the suicides of Las Vegas is that he still did not know what caused them.

It was to Sergeant Tirso Dominguez, therefore, an officer at the Las

John: I'm not sure how I can say this so that you understand, Jim, because it doesn't seem to be getting across to you. But one more time for the record: I am not a journalist; I'm an essayist. OK? And this is a genre that has existed for a few thousand years. (Ever heard of Cicero?) So these "rules" that I'm working under are not mine, but rather were established by writers who recognized a difference between the hard research of journalism and the kind inquiry of mind that characterizes the essay, an inquiry that's propelled by lots of different sources simultaneously—including science, religion, history, myth, politics, nature, and even the imagination. So there's a bit more freedom in essaying than there is in report-age. Although I would also maintain that I haven't changed the gist of what Dominguez said. I've put words in his mouth, certainly, but not ideas. By stating that he "[doesn't] want to be a part of [this] story" Dominguez is essentially saying "no comment." Nothing here has been "manipulated," only interpreted. And yes, I did it for literary effect, which is also something that essayists do and that journalists don't (or aren't supposed to).

Jim: Since I have five more sections to go, maybe you could help me out, as I'm still a little foggy on the rules. Basically it sounds like you're saying that an essayist can write things with arbitrary truth-value and make quotations out of whole cloth that are attributed to real people who live in the real world. Is that right? And if so, isn't that what people call fiction?

John: Have I changed the meaning of anything here, Jim? No. I've just streamlined this quote in order to help things move along a little better, and to create a bit of resonance with neighboring paragraphs. It's what writers do.

Jim: OK, so now I understand. The rules are: There are no rules, just as long as you make it pretty.

John: That's a bullshit interpreptation of what I just said.

Vegas Metropolitan Police Department's Office of Public Information, that I turned for information about Las Vegas suicides. But "I don't have a comment about anything like that," is how Sergeant Dominguez responded to my request for information.

It was from *Reporting on Suicide: Recommendations for the Media and Public Officials,* a pamphlet of guidelines developed by the Centers for Disease Control, that I learned that "'no comment' is not a productive response to media representatives who are covering a suicide story."

It was Eric Darensburg, assignments editor at KLAS Channel 8 in Las

Jim: I thought you were the great defender of people's rights to "interpret"?

"It was from *Reporting on Suicide: Recommendations for the Media and Public Officials*, a pamphlet of guidelines developed by the Centers for Disease Control, that I learned that '"no comment" is not a productive response to media representatives who are covering a suicide story.'" Point of Fact: John "interpreted" the quote in the previous paragraph so that it could "resonate" with the recommendation here about "no comment," and yet he has also "interpreted" the facts in this paragraph too. For example, the actual title of the publication John is quoting from is *Suicide Contagion and the Reporting of Suicide: Recommendations from a National Workshop*—not, as John has it, *Reporting on Suicide.* Also, the exact quote from the manual is: "'No comment' is not a productive response to media representatives who are covering a suicide story." So his "interpreting" is a little out of control.

John: I streamlined it, that's all.

Jim: Well then your "streamlining" is out of control.

"It was Eric Darensburg, assignments editor at KLAS Channel 8 in Las Vegas, who told me that his station had a policy against recording footage of suicide scenes when I asked to see the footage that his station had recorded of the scene outside the Stratosphere on the evening Levi died. And it was Eric Darensburg who also said, when I provided him with the date on which his station aired that footage, that their film librarian was out of town, that their library was currently very messy, that he wasn't going to be able to track any footage down." The February 21, 2000, "Business Calendar" section of the *Las Vegas Review-Journal* confirms that KLAS is Channel 8, that Darensburg is the "assignments editor," and that his name is spelled correctly. In John's notes there is evidence of an interview in which Darensburg details the station's "policy of not televising" suicide, and of John insisting that he saw this footage on TV. However, there is no mention in John's notes of a "messy library"—only that Darensburg would "have to look around/call later," and then a note that he never did.

"It was from Bob Gerye, principal of the Las Vegas Academy of International Studies and Performing and Visual Arts . . ." Principal's name and title confirmed, as is the school itself, in a photocopied letter from the principal addressed to parents, students, and community members that was in John's notes. The school is a magnet school in downtown Las Vegas. However, the official title of the school is "Las Vegas Academy of International Studies, Visual and Performing Arts." There's an extra "and" between "International Studies" and "Performing" that John has added, plus he's inverted "Performing" and "Visual," for some reason.

John: I altered that, yes, but I would say for the better. The name of the school is too clunky. It has a comma in it; that's ridiculous.

". . . where Levi was a student for two years before he died . . ." Confirmed by some of the photocopies of Levi's school papers that John provided. But I can't confirm that Levi was in attendance at the school for "two years" before he died. He was sixteen, though, so mathematically it's probable.

Vegas, who told me that his station had a policy against recording footage of suicide scenes when I asked to see the footage that his station had recorded of the scene outside the Stratosphere on the evening Levi died. And it was Eric Darensburg who also said, when I provided him with the date on which his station aired that footage, that their film librarian was out of town, that their library was currently very messy, that he wasn't going to be able to track any footage down.

It was from Bob Gerye, principal of the Las Vegas Academy of International Studies and Performing and Visual Arts, where Levi was a student for two years before he died, that I received no comment in response to my request for his insights into the effect of suicide on his school. But it was Bob Gerye who did say, in response to the teachers and parents and students who requested that a memorial be held at their school, "No."

"I don't want," the principal said, "mass hysteria on my hands."

And it was an eyewitness to Levi's death at the Stratosphere Hotel—a man

". . . I received no comment in response to my request for his insights about the effect of suicide on his school." There is no record of any such comment in John's notes, which means that there is technically no record of a "no comment" comment—so it's possible that there was no comment and John didn't see the need to comment on that in his notes. (No comment.)

"But it was Bob Gerye who did say, in response to the teachers and parents and students who requested that a memorial be held at their school, 'No.'" John's notes refer to something like this, but its source is unclear. From what I can tell, it looks like Levi's mom is reporting what the principal said to her. We can probably let it pass.

"'I don't want,' the principal said, 'mass hysteria on my hands.'" The actual quote in John's notes is: "I didn't want mass hysteria in the senior class."

"And it was an eyewitness to Levi's death at the Stratosphere Hotel—a man who'd made a statement to the police that same night, plus several informal statements to various TV stations, one local Vegas blogger, and a weekly tabloid paper—who said to me 'fuck off' when I asked him for a comment." There's nothing about this guy anywhere in John's notes. John, who is this guy? Where is he in your notes? Could I contact him to confirm this exchange?

John: He told me to fuck off. You're not going to get much out of him.

Jim: OK, but my job is to at least try. What's this guy's real name so I can make the attempt?

John: I'm not in the habit of giving out the identities of sources who specifically ask to remain anonymous.

Jim: That's right, I forgot about your hard-core journalistic ethics. Is there any way you can show me some sort of evidence of this source's existence, then? What if I promise to keep whatever you show me confidential and only use it to report back to the magazine that I saw evidence of this guy existing and can confirm your exchange with him?

John: Nope.

west (1994), *On Rims & Ridges: The Los Alamos Area Since 1880* (1992) and *Preserving Different Pasts: The American National Monuments* (1989) as well as the editor of *The Culture of Tourism, the Tourism of Culture* (2003), winner of the Border Regional Library Association's Southwest Book Award for 2003 and a Southwest Book Award from the Tucson–Pima County Library for 2003, *Reopening the American West* (1998) and co-editor with Mike Davis of *The Grit Beneath the Glitter: Tales from the Real Las Vegas* (2002) and with Char Miller, of *Out of the Woods: Essays in Environmental History* (1997)." But there's one major flaw: Rothman is dead. He died in 2007 of Lou Gehrig's disease. John makes it sound like the guy's still around. Plus, isn't it in poor taste to go after a guy like this after he's died? (See below.)

"'This is a private matter,' said the man, hanging up." Again, no evidence.

"'The only real problem Las Vegas faces,' said cultural critic Hal Rothman, the chair of the Department of History at the University of Nevada . . .'" Name, title, and university affiliation can be found on Rothman's homepage on the University of Nevada's website. This is off-topic, but his publications read like a laundry list of books with terrible academic title-colon-subtitle titles: "Hal K. Rothman is Professor of History at the University of Nevada–Las Vegas. Considered one of the nation's leading expert [*sic*] on tourism and post-industrial economies, he is the author of the widely acclaimed *Neon Metropolis: How Las Vegas Shed Its Stigma to Become the First City of the Twenty-First Century* (2002), *Devil's Bargains: Tourism in the Twentieth-Century American West* (1998), which received the 1999 Western Writers of America Spur Award for Contemporary Nonfiction, *Saving the Planet: The American Response to the Environment in the Twentieth Century* (2000), *LBJ's Texas White House: 'Our Heart's Home'* (2001), which received the Award of Merit for 2002 from the Texas Philosophical Society, *The Greening of a Nation?: Environmentalism in the U.S. Since 1945* (1997), *'I'll Never Fight Fire With My Bare Hands Again': Recollections of the First Forest Rangers of the Inland North-*

who'd made a statement to the police that same night, plus several informal statements to various TV stations, one local Vegas blogger, and a weekly tabloid paper—who said to me "fuck off" when I asked him for a comment.

"This is a private matter," said the man, hanging up.

"The only real problem Las Vegas faces," said cultural critic Hal Rothman, the chair of the Department of History at the University of Nevada, is "people who come from other places who don't know shit about this town but want to write about it."

". . . is 'people who come from other places who don't know shit about this town but want to write about it.'" This is taken from the book on Las Vegas that Rothman co-edited with Mike Davis entitled *The Grit Beneath the Glitter*. However, the quote is not precise. The real quote (which appears in the introduction to the book, written by both Davis and Rothman, and yet referring to Rothman in the third person) is: "No wonder that when asked by a group of visiting journalists what the biggest problem Las Vegas faced was, Hal Rothman responded: 'People who come from other places who don't know shit about the town and want to write about it!'" So, first of all, the statement should not be in the second person, as John is using it. Second of all, he didn't say that it was the "only real problem" Las Vegas faced—which would have been a preposterous statement in and of itself, considering that Rothman has written about Vegas and clearly knows what's wrong with the place. So this is a misrepresentation. Plus, the man is dead. I think John should consider being a little more respectful. (*The Grit Beneath the Glitter: Tales from the Real Las Vegas,* ed. Hal Rothman and Mike Davis, University of California Press, 2002.)

"The 'people' to whom Rothman was speaking when he said this were fifteen young journalists from Berkeley, California, who had come to Las Vegas, as Rothman suspected, in order to write a series of essays about the place, a project that resulted in a book entitled _The Real Las Vegas: Life Beyond the Strip_ . . ." Confirmation that some Berkeley students visited Las Vegas to write this book can be found in "Outsiders Looking In," an undated article in _Gambling Magazine._ But in the introduction to the Rothman book mentioned above, it is not specified that Rothman was actually talking to these particular Berkeley students. Also, there are fourteen essays in this book, aside from the introduction, which was written by the professor. So, even though we don't know if there were more students than essays published, the best guess would be that there were "fourteen young journalists" rather than "fifteen young journalists," since I doubt that the professor would want to be grouped in with the youngsters. In addition, these students were in a graduate journalism program at Berkeley, so how "young" could they be? This makes it sound like they were in high school or something.

". . . a collection of hard-hitting cultural criticism that has since been called one of the most insightful portraits of the city since _Learning from Las Vegas_." The Berkeley book is indeed long-form cultural criticism. And there is indeed a book entitled _Learning from Las Vegas,_ which was written by Robert Venturi, Steven Izenour, and Denise Scott Brown. Although from the looks of it _Learning from Las Vegas_ is mostly

The "people" to whom Rothman was speaking when he said this were fifteen young journalists from Berkeley, California, who had come to Las Vegas, as Rothman suspected, in order to write a series of essays about the place, a project that resulted in a book entitled _The Real Las Vegas: Life Beyond the Strip,_ a collection of hard-hitting cultural criticism that has since been called one of the most insightful portraits of the city since _Learning from Las Vegas_. It was published around the same time as Rothman's own study, _Neon Metropolis: How Las Vegas Shed Its Stigma to Become the First City of the Twenty-First Century,_ a book of conspicuously aggressive boosterism for a work of supposed criticism, a combination of cultural pandering and pro-business rallying from an author who seems never to have met a corporate shark he didn't like.

Indeed, that "shit about the town" which Rothman insists only locals like himself are allowed to write is seldom actually written about by Las Vegas locals.

"Another sign of how much America's

about architecture. So I'm not sure John's comparing apples and apples here. Also, I can't find any reference to the Berkeley students' book being referred to as "one of the most insightful portraits of the city" since _Learning from Las Vegas._ Source?

> John: According to me it's the most insightful.
> Jim: Ah . . . convenient.

". . . published around the same time as Rothman's own study, _Neon Metropolis: How Las Vegas Shed Its Stigma to Become the First City of the Twenty-First Century_ . . ." Title confirmed on Rothman's University of Nevada homepage. However, these two books were not "published around the same time," as John states. They appeared three years apart; the Berkeley book in 1999 and Rothman's in 2002.

". . . a book of conspicuously aggressive boosterism for a work of supposed criticism, a combination of cultural pandering and pro-business rallying from an author who seems never to have met a corporate shark he didn't like." Description of author/ book: This is obviously John's personal take on the book, but it's worth noting that based on other reviews of the text, John's is by no means a fringe opinion.

"'Another sign of how much America's fastest growing city has become hostage to the corporate lords of gambling,' Sally Denton wrote in a December 2000 article in the _Columbia Journalism Review_." Name, publication, issue, and at least this portion of the quote are accurate. However, the article was written by both Sally Denton and a guy named Roger Morris, who went on to co-write an entire book about this issue: *The Money and the Power: The Making of Las Vegas and Its Hold on America*. No clue why John dropped the credit for Morris.

"**"This situation seems borne out by the number of local reporters who, like elected politicians and public officials, tend to end up on the public relations staffs of Las Vegas casinos.'"** This part of the quote is flawed. It actually should read: "The judgment seems borne out by the number of local reporters, who, like elected politicians and public officials, tend to end up on the public relations staffs of casinos."

John: The article is about Las Vegas, so "Las Vegas" is implied in that sentence. However, since I'm using the sentence out of context I wanted to make sure that the reader knew for sure that it was *Las Vegas* casinos that were being referred to. So I plugged in "Las Vegas."

Jim: John, that's what brackets are for: ". . . tend to end up on the public relations staffs of [Las Vegas] casinos."

John: I know that's what they're for, Jim. I went to high school, too. I just think brackets are ugly.

Jim: You're misquoting if you don't enclose "Las Vegas" in brackets.

John: I'm not misquoting. No borderline-intelligent person could read that sentence in its original context and not understand that the casinos being referred to are Las Vegas casinos. There is no manipulation occurring there whatsoever.

Jim: It'll end up making your research techniques look sloppy, though.

John: And I think that brackets will make the sentence look "sloppy," so I guess we're at a standoff.

fastest growing city has become hostage to the corporate lords of gambling," Sally Denton wrote in a December 2000 article in the *Columbia Journalism Review*. "This situation seems borne out by the number of local reporters who, like elected politicians and public officials, tend to end up on the public relations staffs of Las Vegas casinos."

In 1983, for example, when Las Vegas casino owner Steve Wynn decided to apply for a gaming license in Britain, *The Independent* of London reported that an investigation by Scotland Yard drew links between Wynn and the Genovese crime family, an investigation that was subsequently referred to in advertisements by the publisher of a new book about Steve Wynn, *Running Scared: The Life and Treacherous Times of Las Vegas Casino King Steve Wynn*. However, even though the *Independent*'s report was never challenged, Wynn still

"**In 1983, for example, when Las Vegas casino owner Steve Wynn decided to apply for a gaming license in Britain, *The Independent* of London reported that an investigation by Scotland Yard drew links between Wynn and the Genovese crime family . . .**" According ing to the *Columbia Journalism Review*, *The Independent* reported about this Scotland Yard file in a March 2000 article. *The Independent* didn't report about it when it happened in 1983. So the statement as written is chronologically misleading.

"**. . . an investigation that was subsequently referred to in advertisements by the publisher of a new book about Steve Wynn, *Running Scared: The Life and Treacherous Times of Las Vegas Casino King Steve Wynn*.**" Most of this is confirmed by the *Columbia Journalism Review*. But the original publication date of *Running Scared* was 1995, so it's not particularly "new." John, do you mean "recent"? Also, wouldn't the link between Steve Wynn and the Genovese family have been made by the author of the book, rather than the publisher?

John: The link was made in an advertisement that the publisher issued about the book—just as the sentence states. The author didn't do his own advertising, and neither did he make this link in the book itself. The statement is accurate as it is written.

"**However, even though the *Independent*'s report was never challenged, Wynn still sued the publisher of *Running Scared* for what he considered 'libelous statements,' winning $3 million in a Nevada state court, bankrupting the publisher of the biography in question, and somehow winning support from**"

Las Vegas journalists, such that the allegations that initiated his suit were covered by the daily *Las Vegas Review-Journal*—arguably the most influential paper in the state—for only one day, in only one article, on page five, section B, under the quarter-inch-high headline 'Wynn Sues Local Writer.'" I haven't bothered trying to confirm whether this was in fact the size of the headline, but we can allow for some artistic license here, especially since it seems to be more effort than it's worth, given the extreme unlikeliness that John will budge on this. But Factual Dispute: Wynn actually won $3.1 million in the settlement, not "$3 million."

"In contrast, the *Las Vegas Review-Journal* provided several weeks' worth of coverage for Las Vegas mayor Oscar Goodman when he threatened to sue a writer named James McManus, an Illinois reporter whose popular memoir, *Positively Fifth Street*, falsely alleged the mayor's participation in planning the assassination of a local judge . . ." Goodman was indeed the mayor of Las Vegas at that time, as the city's website confirms.

"'With Jimmy Chagra on trial in Texas for heroin trafficking, Jack, Ted, and Benny Binion convened in booth no. 1 of the

sued the publisher of *Running Scared* for what he considered "libelous statements," winning $3 million in a Nevada state court, bankrupting the publisher of the biography in question, and somehow winning support from Las Vegas journalists, such that the allegations that initiated his suit were covered by the daily *Las Vegas Review-Journal*—arguably the most influential paper in the state—for only one day, in only one article, on page five, section B, under the quarter-inch-high headline "Wynn Sues Local Writer."

In contrast, the *Las Vegas Review-Journal* provided several weeks' worth of coverage for Las Vegas mayor Oscar Goodman when he threatened to sue a writer named James McManus, an Illinois reporter whose popular memoir, *Positively Fifth Street*, falsely alleged the mayor's participation in planning the assassination of a local judge:

> With Jimmy Chagra on trial in Texas for heroin trafficking, Jack, Ted, and Benny Binion convened in booth no. 1 of the Horseshoe Coffee Shop with Oscar Goodman, the hyper-aggressive young attorney representing the accused. The upshot of that meeting was a $50,000 contract for Charles Harrelson, actor Woody's father, to assassinate U.S. District Judge John Wood—or so the lore has had it.

While the lore surrounding Las Vegas mayor Oscar Goodman has always had it that actor Woody's father

Horseshoe Coffee Shop with Oscar Goodman, the hyper-aggressive young attorney representing the accused. The upshot of that meeting was a $50,000 contract for Charles Harrelson, actor Woody's father, to assassinate U.S. District Judge John Wood—or so the lore has had it.'" Quotation Accuracy: The book places a lot of these names in parentheses, presumably because the full names are meant to be implied: "With (Jimmy) Chagra on trial . . ."; "Jack, Ted, and Benny (Binion) convened . . ."; and "for Charles Harrelson (actor Woody's father) to assassinate . . ." It's a misquote to not retain the original parentheses.

"While the lore surrounding Las Vegas mayor Oscar Goodman has always had it that actor Woody's father was indeed once hired, that Judge John Wood was indeed once murdered, that Mayor Oscar Goodman did indeed defend Chagra, and indeed that his defense of other Las Vegas figures whom residents widely recognize as members of the mob was the kind of back-scratching that helped employ the mayor before his election . . ." All of this can be found in John L. Smith's book *Of Rats and Men*, an excerpt of which was published in the *Las Vegas Review-Journal* on September 21, 2003. The book is more or less one long case for why Goodman loves the mob and the mob loves him. From the book: "Oscar Goodman admits he finds rays of hope under the darkest circumstances. It was that way in the case of the U.S. vs. Jamiel 'Jimmy' Chagra. Chagra was accused of obstructing justice, conspiring to distribute a small mountain of marijuana, conspiracy to commit murder, and murder itself (the assassination of San Antonio federal Judge John Wood) . . . It wasn't a murder-for-hire plot, Goodman proposed, but extortion after the fact. Hit man Charles Harrelson (father of actor Woody Harrelson) saw Chagra as a mark, as evidenced by his attempt to con him out of several hundred thousand dollars in a rigged poker game in Las Vegas, and the Wood assassination was Harrelson's chance for the score of a lifetime." So if it wasn't lore before the book was published, it certainly became so afterward.

was indeed once hired, that Judge John Wood was indeed once murdered, that Mayor Oscar Goodman did indeed defend Chagra, and indeed that his defense of other Las Vegas figures whom residents widely recognize as members of the mob was the kind of back-scratching that helped employ the mayor before his election, that meeting at the Horseshoe as described by McManus could not be proven as having ever taken place, which is why, as the *Las Vegas Review-Journal* wrote about the suit, "the Mayor took offense at this besmirching of his name," and which is why, as the *Las Vegas Review-Journal* subsequently wrote, "Mayor Oscar Goodman may have defended reputed mobsters, but that doesn't mean he is one," and which is why, as the *Las Vegas Review-Journal* also later wrote, "ironies abound in Goodman's life . . . here's a man who freely admits his acquaintance with casino Black Book members and crime family capos . . . and here is a man who demands respect," and which is why, as the *Las Vegas Review-Journal* finally explained, "not only was the allegation that Goodman was included in a criminal conspiracy without factual basis, it

". . . that meeting at the Horseshoe as described by McManus could not be proven as having ever taken place, which is why, as the *Las Vegas Review-Journal* wrote about the suit, 'the Mayor took offense at this besmirching of his name' . . ." The actual quote is: "The mayor took offense at the besmirching of his rep— which is Goodman's part-time avocation, so long as he's the only one doing the besmirching—and threatened to sue" ("Truth and the Media" by Steve Sebelius, *Las Vegas Review-Journal,* June 12, 2003).

John: "Name," "rep" . . . what's the difference?

". . . and which is why, as the *Las Vegas Review-Journal* subsequently wrote, 'Mayor Oscar Goodman may have defended reputed mobsters, but that doesn't mean he is one'. . ." Actual quote: "Mayor Oscar Goodman may have defended reputed mobsters in court. But he wanted the world to know he wasn't one."

John: Again, same gist.

". . . and which is why, as the *Las Vegas Review-Journal* also later wrote, 'ironies abound in Goodman's life . . . here's a man who freely admits his acquaintance with casino Black Book members and crime family capos . . . and here is a man who demands respect' . . ." Actual quote: "Ironies abound in Goodman's life. One obvious one emerged Tuesday afternoon in his City Hall Office as he addressed reporters: Here's a man who freely admits his acquaintance with casino Black Book members and crime family capos while at the same time fiercely defending his reputation. Here's a man who demands respect . . ."

John: Again, the gist is there. I've just clear-cut the gobbledygook out of the quote.

". . . and which is why, as the *Las Vegas Review-Journal* finally explained, 'not only was the allegation that Goodman was included in a criminal conspiracy without factual basis, it wasn't the only error in the paragraph. The dominant subject of the paragraph, Jimmy Chagra, was called a heroin trafficker, but in reality he worked with cocaine.'" Actual quote: "Not only was the allegation that Goodman was involved in a criminal conspiracy without factual basis, it wasn't the only error in the paragraph. The dominant subject of the paragraph, Jimmy Chagra, was called a heroin trafficker, but in reality he worked with cocaine and marijuana." John seems to want the ironic force of that "cocaine," but unfortunately it's inaccurate to end the sentence there ("Inaccuracies Don't Impair Sales of Book That Led to Goodman Complaint" by John L. Smith, *Las Vegas Review-Journal,* June 13, 2003).

John: Why is it inaccurate? I'm just trimming off the mention of marijuana in order to help the sentence end more forcefully. It's not like if we allowed "marijuana" to stay there—dangling awkwardly off the end of that sentence—we would change the sentence's meaning or make the guy look any better or worse. I have to say, I really do not see the point of this kind of "accuracy." The real point of that sentence is the comparison between heroin and coke.

". . . within a few weeks, in the *New York Times*

wasn't the only error in the paragraph. The dominant subject of the paragraph, Jimmy Chagra, was called a heroin trafficker, but in reality he worked with cocaine."

In the end, this was local coverage that so triumphantly succeeded for Mayor Oscar Goodman that within a few weeks, in the *New York Times Book Review,* a full-page ad appeared with a letter of apology addressed to Mayor Goodman, signed by the publisher of McManus's book. It was accompanied by a photograph featuring Mayor Goodman, arms folded, face smiling, legs spread and firmly braced beneath the shiny glass hull of the Stratosphere Hotel.

"We don't want anything in our city that might upset the tourist," State Senator Dina Titus has said about her district, the seventh precinct of Clark County, Las Vegas, Nevada. "So if it's a touch of reality that isn't pretty, then we want to get rid of it. You don't want to come in contact with reality when you're here for a fantasy."

Book Review, a full-page ad appeared with a letter of apology addressed to Mayor Goodman, signed by the publisher of McManus's book. It was accompanied by a photograph featuring Mayor Goodman, arms folded, face smiling, legs spread and firmly braced beneath the shiny glass hull of the Stratosphere Hotel." Description of ad confirmed in a *Las Vegas Review-Journal* article, aptly titled "Full-Page Apology to Goodman Appears in *New York Times,*" which was published July 8, 2003.

"'We don't want anything in our city that might upset the tourist,'" State Senator Dina Titus has said about her district, the seventh precinct of Clark County, Las Vegas, Nevada. 'So if it's a touch of reality that isn't pretty, then we want to get rid of it. You don't want to come in contact with reality when you're here for a fantasy.'" Confirmed: It's a quote from *Las Vegas: An Unconventional History,* a documentary about the city that aired on PBS as part of their *American Experience* series in 2005.

5

"'**Well of course people are paranoid about suicide here,' Ron Flud explained in his County Coroner's Office.**" Problem: According to the Clark County Coroner's website, Ron Flud is no longer the coroner. Someone named P. Michael Murphy is. Flud is mentioned as the former coroner in an article I found in the *Las Vegas Review-Journal,* however ("Clark County Coroner Rules That French Inmate Died of Asphyxia" by Ryan Oliver, *Las Vegas Review-Journal,* February 13, 2001). I suggest John change this to "the former coroner" or "the then-coroner."

John: "The then-coroner"? Is that a joke?

"**. . . Ron Flud was the only official in Greater Las Vegas who agreed to talk about suicide.**" I can't confirm whether or not he was the "only" official who would talk. But John's notes do show signs of intense frustration with lots of folks who turned down his requests for interviews.

"'**I'm a finder of facts,' he said, 'that's my job, it's what I do. I don't see the point of concealing information.'**" Another Problem: I actually don't see any evidence of this conversation with Flud in John's notes. I mean, anywhere. I see a notation for "1:00 p.m.—lunch—Olive Garden, Ron Flud/office," but no evidence of that conversation actually taking place. Maybe this was one of John's "casual" interviews.

"**The Coroner's Office in Las Vegas is tan and stuccoed and flat-roofed and small and wedged within a**

"Well of course people are paranoid about suicide here," Ron Flud explained in his County Coroner's Office. "I mean, it's in business, it needs tourists. Every resident's bread and butter is based on this city's image. And suicide doesn't sell."

Indeed, Ron Flud was the only official in Greater Las Vegas who agreed to talk about suicide.

"I'm a finder of facts," he said, "that's my job, it's what I do. I don't see the point of concealing information."

The Coroner's Office in Las Vegas is tan and stuccoed and flat-roofed and small and wedged within a district of attorneys' offices and accountants' offices and psychiatrists' offices and banks. Inside it are no blood-spotted sheets covering bodies in the lobby or tumblers lying around full of cloudy yellow liquids, no people in the hallways wearing black rubber aprons or walking to and fro wielding shiny silver tools. In

district of attorneys' offices and accountants' offices and psychiatrists' offices and banks." John's notes also don't offer any evidence of him trying to find this office. However, based on an online satellite picture of downtown Las Vegas, it does appear to be in the vicinity of a number of attorneys/accountants/banks/psychiatrists, and it does look to be flat-roofed, although I can't confirm its stucconess. However, it's a freestanding building with a parking lot around it, placed amongst other freestanding buildings with parking lots around them, so I'm not sure we could characterize the building as being "wedged" within anything.

"**Inside it are no blood-spotted sheets covering bodies in the lobby or tumblers lying around full of cloudy yellow liquids, no people in the hallways wearing black rubber aprons or walking to and fro wielding shiny silver tools.**" This statement is hard to approach. Is he implying that the Coroner's Office didn't look like this when he visited at that particular point in time? Or that it never looks like this, and that it wouldn't ever look this way? I guess either way, those scenarios do seem pretty unlikely, although I can't prove that they never happened.

John: Huh? It means that I didn't see any of that shit while I was there—that it's a plain-looking office, in other words. It's meant to be an obvious and amusing statement. Of course there wouldn't be bodies lying around . . . jeez.

"... is a small sign in the lobby—ATTENTION FUNERAL DIRECTORS—a plaque from Nellis Air Force Base—IN GRATITUDE FOR YOUR SER-VICE—and someone's remark to a secretary as he passed her in a rush—'Thank you for the chocolate coffin, Pam.'" No notes on this either. Sensing a pattern here? These days the secretary there is named "Nicole." But I guess "Pam" sounds like a reasonable name for a Coroner's Office secretary with a morbid sense of humor. Is that why he changed it?

"'I think everyone's a lot more comfortable,' Ron said ..." Hey, for what it's worth, not keeping blood-splattered corpses in your lobby gets you halfway there. But anyway, I don't know what to do here—none of this is in his notes.

"There was in fact no word for it in the ancient Greek language. There was never one in Hebrew, never one in Latin, no word for it in Chinese." Factual Dispute: In Greek and Latin, there were definitely terms for suicide; there just weren't any root words for them. I emailed a friend of mine who is a graduate student in linguistics at Harvard, and he sent me the following explanation: "That writer you're quoting is technically right, because both classical languages have only transparent compounds or transparent verbal phrases with a reflexive pronoun—so a standard Latin example would be: *mihi mortem consisco,* 'incur death to myself,' or in Greek: *apotassomai toi bioi,* 'set [oneself] apart from life.' Additionally, Greek also has only nominal compounds that can be construed with 'oneself': *autokheir,* which literally means 'having one's own hands to oneself.' So my point is, yes, technically speaking, both classical idioms lack a root with the basic meaning of 'suicide' (whereby of course it should be mentioned that *suicide,* being a Latin LW, was a compound in Latin 'to kill oneself,' *sui + caedo*). But nevertheless, it would still be a misstatement to say that Latin and Greek have 'no words' for suicide. Romans and Greeks could certainly express the idea

fact, the only indications that his office is responsible for determining the cause of death of nearly everyone in Vegas is a small sign in the lobby—ATTENTION FUNERAL DIRECTORS—a plaque from Nellis Air Force Base—IN GRATITUDE FOR YOUR SERVICE—and someone's remark to a secretary as he passed her in a rush—"Thank you for the chocolate coffin, Pam."

"I think everyone's a lot more comfortable," Ron said, "if we keep a low profile here."

There was in fact no word for it in the ancient Greek language.

if they wanted to." In addition to that explanation, according to the website *Etymology Online,* there is indeed a word for suicide in modern Church Latin: *suicidium,* which means "deliberate killing of oneself," which derives from the Proto-Indo-European *s(w)e,* which means "one's self," and *cidium,* which means "a killing." In addition, the use of another term, *felo-de-se,* dates back to 1728 and literally means "one guilty concerning himself," and was frequently used to describe suicide. So the point is that there were words for suicide. John, can you clarify what you're meaning by there being "no words" for suicide?

John: Well, first of all, "Church Latin," as you call it, is Vulgate Latin, and Vulgate Latin is bullshit. It emerged about a thousand years after the Romans of antiquity existed. But I'm not sure what your point is anyway, because according to your Harvard buddy I'm correct.

Jim: Moving on: For Chinese, there are also issues. Presumably John's talking about Mandarin here? Chinese is a language family, so there is no single "Chinese language." Rather, "Chinese" is a family of closely related but for the most part mutually unintelligible languages, of which Mandarin, or "Modern Standard Chinese," is the most common, and what people are often referring to when they talk about "Chinese." This is from an email from Matt Rutherford, another buddy who was a grad student at the big H in Middle Eastern Studies: "Dear Jiminy, The word for suicide in Chinese (Mandarin) is *zi-sha*—two characters. *zi* means 'to oneself' (i.e.: reflexive) and *sha* means 'to kill.' So, *zi-sha* means to 'kill oneself.' Now, technically, it is true that there is no single character that means 'suicide.' Chinese has to say it reflexively like Greek. However, I'm not sure whether it's correct to read things into this. Chinese has lots of words that can only be represented with combinations of characters. You could argue that the Chinese word for hanging (i.e.: as a form of punishment) is *gua-si,* literally 'hang-death,' and that since there is no inherent single word for hanging as a punishment then the Chinese don't believe in capital punishment. But that would be patently untrue, of course, as China kills more prisoners than any other country in the world. So *zi-sha* (suicide) is a perfectly common grammatical formulation in Chinese, and this reflexive form is seen in many other instances. The fact that there isn't a single character to express the meaning is true, but any cultural inferences from this would be wrong. Still, if the guy wants to infer, let him infer. Poetic license and all. However, I just want to make it clear that there is a common word for suicide in Chinese, and that suicide has been around in China for thousands of years. (Emperors were known to hang themselves from trees when their dynasties were about to be defeated by invading hordes, for example.)" But as far as Hebrew goes, I'm not so certain. John, any source for this? I consulted a number of dictionaries and wasn't able to find it, and I also couldn't get a response from any of my Harvard linguistics buddies on this one.

John: Hmm, not sure. Maybe somebody at Yale knows. Or Dartmouth? Did you try Dartmouth?

Jim: All right, whatever.

"And until three hundred years ago, there wasn't one in English either." Factual Dispute: According to *Etymology Online*, the English use of the word "suicide" dates back to 1651, which is more than three hundred fifty years ago.

"'I think that's because suicide is the most threatening thing that we can encounter as a culture,' Ron said." Again, I couldn't find this statement in John's notes. However, the sentiment does seem to follow Flud's other comments about suicide in the local papers. But, there is a problem with the causation that's implied here between language influencing how people think, and vice versa. For example, if "that's because" (in the first line of Flud's statement) refers to the linguistics point, this is treading on unsteady

There was never one in Hebrew, never one in Latin, no word for it in Chinese.

And until three hundred years ago, there wasn't one in English either.

"I think that's because suicide is the most threatening thing that we can encounter as a culture," Ron said. "It's a manifestation of doubt, the ultimate unknowable. A suicide by someone we know—or even by someone we don't know—is an ugly reminder that none of us has the answers. So apply that to a city with the nation's most frequent suicides and you might start to understand this city's reluctance to talk about it."

ground. It's an invocation of some sort of reverse form of linguistic determinism (i.e., something like the Sapir-Whorf hypothesis, the theory that "there is a systematic relationship between the grammatical categories of the language a person speaks and how that person both understands the world and behaves in it"), going either from the structure of language to the way people think or the way people think to the structure of language. This is shaky at best, especially given that the languages we've talked about clearly do have concepts of and terms for suicide. And making broad conclusions about a group of people based on the structure of their language is pretty suspect. It's still something that is under debate by linguists, and there are theories that support both sides, but even with that aside, this kind of general statement ignores the massive and complex cultural baggage—positive and negative—that suicide has had attached to it in other eras and in other cultures. The point that Flud allegedly makes (that people are ashamed of suicide-as-disorder) seems limited to suicides by the depressed vs. the Hellenistic or East Asian warrior traditions of suicide as an honorable way to surrender, or even other cultural uses for suicide, such as suicide as an atonement, or suicide as an act of protest, or as a philosophical statement, or as the noble self-destructive act of a terminally ill person. So, source for this idea, John?

John: Wow, Jim, your penis must be so much bigger than mine.

Jim: Excuse me?

John: Your job is to fact-check me, Jim, not my subjects.

Jim: No need to get juvenile, John. I'm just trying to point out that what he's saying is logically flawed.

John: Then let it be flawed. The quote is helping characterize the subject by offering his take on the cultural phenomenon of suicide. And that's its only point. Whether he's "right" or "wrong" or logically virtuous isn't the point. We would in fact be presenting an inaccurate picture of him if we started correcting his "logic."

Jim: All right, then could we at least verify that you two actually spoke. Because I still can't even find this quote in your notes.

John: I don't know where those notes would be. I gave you what I had. He and I talked a couple times.

"In 533, at the Second Council of Orléans, Catholic cardinals actually voted to 'outlaw' suicide." I found the following in an essay that included a historical profile on attitudes toward suicide: "The second Roman Catholic Council of Orléans (AD 533) expressed the first official disapproval of suicide, considering it (ambiguously) as either the Devil's work or an expression of mental insanity" ("Suicide: Historical, Descriptive, and Epidemiological Considerations" by Leonardo Tondo, M.D., and Ross J. Baldessarini, M.D., *Medscape.com*, March 15, 2001). While my very Catholic mother dissents that cardinals can't "vote to outlaw" things, it actually seems like a reasonable gloss to refer to the Church's institutional disapproval as an "outlawing." However, there is still a complicated semantic issue here. It is more accurate to say that the Council of Orléans was attended by bishops, not cardinals, because being a "cardinal" means that you have an honorary title and that you are an advisor to the Pope and are part of the Pope's electorate. However, in the early Middle Ages, the term referred to any priest permanently attached to a church ("every clericus, either *intitulatus* or *incardinatus*")—so there were cardinal-priests, cardinal-deacons, and cardinal-bishops. While technically the twenty-five bishops who attended the Council of Orléans were also cardinals, within the Church, and within documentation about the Church, the attendees of these early meetings are referred to as "bishops," to disambiguate their official hierarchical positions. (Source: articles on the "Councils of Orléans" and "Cardinal" in the *Catholic Encyclopedia* on *Newadvent .org*.) I would recommend that John change this therefore to "bishops."

John: Jim, seriously. Chill the fuck out.

In 533, at the Second Council of Orléans, Catholic cardinals actually voted to "outlaw" suicide.

The Talmud forbids even mourning its victims.

And before one can ponder Islam's ancient question—"What ought one think of suicide?"—the Koran quickly answers, "It is much worse than homicide."

"The Talmud forbids even mourning its victims." Almost Confirmed: An article on Jewish attitudes toward suicide states: "The Talmud, written and codified during the early Christian era, specifically condemns suicide. The Talmud's condemnation of suicide is based on the interpretation of Genesis 9:5 'For your lifeblood I will surely require a reckoning.' Only self-inflicted deaths under extreme situations were acceptable, such as in apostasy, ignominy, and disgrace of capture or torture. The victim and his family were punished by denial of regular burial and the customary rituals of mourning. The severity of this punishment caused rabbis of the time to consider a self-inflicted death as only that which was announced beforehand and carried out in front of eyewitnesses. Modern Jewish scholars believe that the harsh Jewish treatment of suicide was partly due to the negative Christian influence on the subject" ("The Jewish Attitude Toward Suicide," Ch. W. Reines, *Judaism*, vol. 10, Spring 1966, p. 170).

"And before one can ponder Islam's ancient question—'What ought one think of suicide?'—the Koran quickly answers, 'It is much worse than homicide.'" Professor Charles A. Kimball, Chair of the Department of Religion at Wake Forest University in Winston-Salem, North Carolina, was asked this question during a Q&A on core Muslim beliefs: "What is the Koran's stance on suicide?" His response was: "There is only one verse in the Koran that contains a phrase related to suicide: 'O you who believe! Do not consume your wealth in the wrong way, rather through trade mutually agreed to, and do not kill yourselves. Surely God is Merciful toward you' (4:29). Some commentators believe that this phrase is better translated as 'do not kill each other.' The prophetic tradition, however, clearly prohibits suicide. The hadith materials, which are the authoritative sayings and actions of the prophet Muhammad, includes many unambiguous statements about suicide: one who 'throws himself off a mountain' or 'drinks poison' or 'kills himself with a sharp instrument' will be in the fire of Hell. Suicide is not allowed even to those in extreme conditions such as painful illness or a serious wound. Ultimately, it is

God, not humans, who has authority over the span of a person's life" ("Q&A: Islamic Fundamentalism: A World-Renowned Scholar Explains Key Points of Islam" by Josh Burek and James Norton, *Christian Science Monitor,* October 4, 2001). However, putting "it is much worse than homicide" in quotes is misleading because it implies that this is a direct quote from the Koran. While this assertion makes some sense given the context (it's not explicit, but presumably one can repent a murder, though not a suicide), I would still suggest correcting this passage to read: "the Koran quickly answers that it is much worse than homicide."

"Hindus condemn it . . ." While certainly most mainstream Hindus condemn suicide, not all of them do: "Hinduism is more tolerant of suicide through its belief in reincarnation and the eventual detachment of the soul from the body. Hinduism also accepts ritual suicide by a widow (suttee), as a way to cancel out her husband's sins and to gain honor for their children, but this practice now is rare" ("Suicide: Historical, Descriptive, and Epidemiological Considerations" by Leonardo Tondo, M.D., and Ross J. Baldessarini, M.D., *Medscape.com,* release date: March 15, 2001).

". . . the Buddha always forbade it . . ." From the entry on "Dharma Data: Suicide" in the *BuddhaNet*'s online encyclopedia: "Suicide was a phenomenon that was known to the Buddha. On one occasion a group of monks doing the meditation on the repulsiveness of the body, without proper guidance, became depressed and killed themselves. When informed that the two lovers had killed themselves so that 'they could be together for eternity' the Buddha commented that these actions were based on desire and ignorance. His attitude toward suicide is clear from the Vinaya where

it is an offence for a monk to encourage or assist someone to commit suicide, and thus on a par with murder. Consequently, in Theravada it is considered a breach of the first Precept, motivated by similar mental states as murder (loathing, fear, anger, desire to escape a problem) only directed towards oneself rather than another." So it seems that the Buddha did forbid suicide; however, the online definition goes on to say: "While Mahayana takes a similar attitude to the more common type of suicide, it did encourage suicide for religious motives. The Lotus Sutra and several other Mahayana works praise the burning of one's own body, a sort of human incense stick, as the 'highest offering.' Stories of bodhisattvas giving parts of their body or even their lives, which are immensely popular in Medieval India, gave self-mutilation and suicide legitimacy. During certain periods in Chinese history such practices became so common that the government had to issue edicts against them." So John's technically right that the Buddha himself discouraged suicide; but it looks like Buddhism as an institution has occasionally found it acceptable.

Hindus condemn it, the Buddha always forbade it, and in Zurich there was an ordinance once on the city's books that condemned all suicides to burials beneath a mountain.

"So that their souls," read the law, "may eternally be suppressed."

". . . and in Zurich there was an ordinance once on the city's books that condemned all suicides to burials beneath a mountain." Can't find any reference to this ordinance anywhere. Source?

John: Not sure, but I'm sure I could find it if nailing down this tiny little fact is that important.

Jim: "Important" is relative at this point. But I'd like to have it for the sake of thoroughness.

John: OK, will hunt around.

Jim: Awesome, thank you. And you know, while we've hit some rough patches off and on, I think things are looking pretty good.

John: Sorry, can't find it.

"**Psychologists were still debating the criminality of suicide as late as the 1960s, claiming that women who kill themselves after committing adultery—or, in the professional terminology at the time, 'morally fallen women'—will usually commit suicide by jumping from a window. That gay men who feel ashamed of being 'sexually penetrated' will stab themselves repeatedly until they are dead. Or that anyone who is maddened by 'poisonous thoughts' will likely succumb to gas.**" The period of the 1960s, as well as the phrases "morally fallen women" and "poisonous thoughts," can be confirmed by *The Traitor Within* by Ellis and Allen, published in 1961. But I'm unable to find the reference to gay men feeling ashamed of being "sexually penetrated." (Just imagine the fun I had searching for that one.)

"**'I'd say the taboo surrounding suicide is the number one reason I get sued,' Ron said.**" I've found the part of John's notes that deal with Flud. And this statement is consistent with what Flud seems to have said during his conversations with John. Looks like there were two different sessions with Flud: one that has no accompanying notes, and another that took place in his office with some pretty good notes. I guess their first conversation was the "courtship" and this one was all business.

Psychologists were still debating the criminality of suicide as late as the 1960s, claiming that women who kill themselves after committing adultery—or, in the professional terminology at the time, "morally fallen women"—will usually commit suicide by jumping from a window. That gay men who feel ashamed of being "sexually penetrated" will stab themselves repeatedly until they are dead. Or that anyone who is maddened by "poisonous thoughts" will likely succumb to gas.

"I'd say the taboo surrounding suicide is the number one reason I get sued," Ron said.

Earlier in the week, Ron had been in court for a trial in which a suicide victim's family had sued him in order to change his classification of their only daughter's death.

"Apparently, when I called it a 'suicide' I prevented her from going to heaven."

He scratched his beard and looked away.

"And I understand their motivation, as silly as it seems. The whole cultural psychology of this city is obsessed with convincing ourselves that this is a place of leisure, that no one can get hurt here. But this is a city just like any

"**'Apparently, when I called it a "suicide" I prevented her from going to heaven.'**" John's notes also confirm this anecdote about Flud being sued by a Mormon family to change his classification of their daughter's death. However, there are no direct quotes from Flud about this anecdote. Just the basic story of what went down. So John's "fleshing out" a bit here.

"**He scratched his beard and looked away.**" A photograph of Flud in a *Las Vegas Review-Journal* article entitled "Clark County Coroner Rules That French Inmate Died of Asphyxia" confirms that Flud does indeed sport a beard.

"**'And I understand their motivation, as silly as it seems. The whole cultural psychology of this city is obsessed with convincing ourselves that this is a place of leisure, that no one can get hurt here. But this is a city just like any other city . . . [etc.]'**" The gist of this paragraph more or less is confirmed by John's notes.

other city. We don't live in the hotels, we don't eat dinner at the buffets, our wives and daughters aren't all feather dancers at lounges on the Strip. Las Vegas is a town. And it can be wonderful and it can be fun, but it's also a place with more suicides than anywhere else in America. Now, obviously, I understand why the city doesn't include that in any of its brochures, but my point is that we can't fix the problem if we don't actually start acknowledging it."

Behind Ron Flud in his downtown office was a portrait of George Washington mounted on a horse. A thin brown folder was on his wide polished desk. Inside it, the cause of Levi Presley's death—"multiple head and body traumas"—was typed into the box labeled BODY in his three-page Coroner's Report.

"Anyway," Ron said. "Guess we should move on to why you're really here."

He opened and closed the folder intermittently as we talked, massaging out of it facts before molding them into stories.

He said, for example, after glancing at a photograph of Levi's body after falling, that the worst damage done to a body like this is "internal, not external . . . hard to believe, eh?"

"He said, 'Did you know there's a maximum airspeed our bodies will reach, no matter how high we jump from or how heavy we are?'" Confirmed that there is a "terminal velocity" for human bodies while falling, although what this speed is is not generally agreed upon. It is accepted to be roughly somewhere between 150 m.ph. and 200 m.ph., according to Paul Tipler in *College Physics,* p. 105.

"He told me a story about a woman in New Zealand who fell out of an airplane on a flight over mountains. 'She fell 20,000 feet into a pile of snow, and survived without major damage.'" I am unable to confirm this specific story. However, a *BBC News Magazine* article states: "In January 1972, 22-year-old flight attendant Vesna Vulovic's plane exploded due to a suspected terrorist bomb in the cargo section. Ms Vulovic plummeted 33,000 feet in the tail section of the plane to the snowy slopes of the Czech Republic. Despite serious injuries including two broken legs, Ms Vulovic survived and later said: 'To this day I enjoy traveling and have no fear of flying'" ("Can You Survive a Plane Crash?," by Zoe Smeaton, *BBC News Magazine,* August 11, 2005). This might be the origin of Flud's story—either that or John just heard it wrong, or made it up and then lucked into fabricating a story that actually happened the way he imagined it.

"But he did not say that afternoon in his office, even after I asked him two or three times, whether it is likely to lose consciousness in a fall." No evidence in

He said, "Did you know there's a maximum airspeed our bodies will reach, no matter how high we jump from or how heavy we are?"

He told me a story about a woman in New Zealand who fell out of an airplane on a flight over mountains.

"She fell 20,000 feet into a pile of snow, and survived without major damage."

But he did not say that afternoon in his office, even after I asked him two or three times, whether it is likely to lose consciousness in a fall.

He did not say, as a nineteenth-century geologist who studied mountain climbers once did, that there is "no anxiety, no trace of despair, no pain, no regret, nor any sadness as one falls . . . Instead, the person who is falling often hears beautiful music while surrounded by a superbly blue heaven that is filled with roseate clouds . . . and then, suddenly, and painlessly, all sensations are extinguished immediately from the body at the exact moment that the body makes contact with the ground."

John's notes of him asking Flud this. And certainly not "two or three times."

"He did not say, as a nineteenth-century geologist who studied mountain climbers once did, that there is 'no anxiety, no trace of despair, no pain, no regret, nor any sadness as one falls . . . Instead, the person who is falling often hears beautiful music while surrounded by a superbly blue heaven that is filled with roseate clouds . . . and then, suddenly, and painlessly, all sensations are extinguished immediately from the body at the exact moment that the body makes contact with the ground.'" It's pretty unlikely that Flud referenced an obscure piece of medical writing in his chat with John, since it doesn't seem like he referenced any of this other stuff either. These quotes John is using are from "The Experience of Dying from Falls" by Russel Noyes Jr., M.D., and Roy Kletti, published in *Omega,* vol. 3, 1972, p. 46. But, not unsurprisingly, John is misquoting the article. The first part of the quote does not include the words "no regret" and it also has been altered in other ways: "There was no anxiety, no trace of despair, no pain; but rather seriousness, profound acceptance, and a dominant mental quickness and sense of surety." And then the second quote: ". . . the person falling often heard beautiful music and fell in a superbly blue heaven containing roseate cloudlets." And the third: "Then consciousness was painlessly extinguished, usually at the moment of impact, and the impact was, at the most, heard but never painfully felt."

"In other words, Ron Flud did not explain how it was that Levi's sneakers in the Polaroid he showed me, lying twenty feet on the brick pavement from his body, were knocked off at the moment his body hit the ground . . ." The Report of Investigation confirms that a "pair of white athletic shoes [were] lying close to the body." So they were off Presley's feet. But I find it extremely unlikely that that they were "twenty feet" from his body if the report says that they were "close." A Polaroid seems like an unlikely medium to take official police pictures in, too. It's also a little suspicious that the coroner would actually show this kind of photograph to a journalist (or whatever John's claiming to be).

In other words, Ron Flud did not explain how it was that Levi's sneakers in the Polaroid he showed me, lying twenty feet on the brick pavement from his body, were knocked off at the moment that his body hit the ground, even though his sneakers look unscuffed in the photo, unstained, still laced, and even double-knotted.

". . . even though his sneakers look unscuffed in the photo, unstained, still laced, and even double-knotted." There is no mention in the Report of Investigation that the sneakers were peculiarly "unscuffed," "unstained," "still laced," or "double-knotted." Maybe John examined this "Polaroid" much more closely than the investigators did. Hey, doesn't the original *CSI* series take place in Vegas? Maybe John could put his crack forensic skills to use as a "(very) creative consultant."

6

"'I wanted to leave my mark on this city,' casino owner Bob Stupak once said about his Stratosphere . . ." Confirmed by John L. Smith in *No Limit: The Rise and Fall of Bob Stupak and Las Vegas' Stratosphere Tower,* Huntington Press, 1997, pp. 142–44.

". . . the tallest American building west of the Mississippi." Confirmed by John Galtant in "Stupak Sets Sights on Steel Tower," *Las Vegas Review-Journal,* October 5, 1989.

"'What I wanted to do for Vegas is what the Eiffel Tower did for Paris, or what the Empire State Building did for New York . . . I wanted my building to be a symbol, to be synonymous with Vegas itself." From the Smith book again, p. 143.

"'Indeed,' said Dave Hickey . . ." This is in John's notes, which indicate that he spoke with Hickey in the "Fireside Lounge in the Peppermill Restaurant, Vegas, December 15, 2002." But the website of the Peppermill makes it seem like the whole place is called just "Peppermill," with the lounge and restaurant given equal billing. So this should actually be called the "Peppermill Fireside Lounge."

". . . an art critic at the University of Nevada in Las Vegas." It's indeed true that the MacArthur-winning "Bad Boy of Art Criticism," who was buddy-buddy with Mapplethorpe, is based out of UNLV. He teaches English there, so technically he's an English professor at UNLV, but I guess technically he is also an art critic . . . who is at UNLV. However, he will not be a resident there for much longer—he and his wife are moving to New Mexico because his wife, Libby Lumpkin, has been appointed a tenured professor in art history at the University of New Mexico. Hickey will actually teach art there, so soon he'll more properly be "an art critic at the University of New Mexico" ("Couple's Exit Leaving Void in Vegas Art Scene," *Las Vegas Sun*). But, he was at UNLV at the time of the interview, so we can probably let this slide.

"Dave Hickey has been called the city's resident art historian, an ambassador for Las Vegas to the rest of the world." I think this is another one of those instances in which John is the one who is calling him this. Ergo, since John has called him that, Hickey has in fact "been called the city's resident art historian." Fine.

"'You know why I like it here?' he said. 'Because everything in this city is economically driven. And that's the only true democracy there is in this country. That's why I like teaching art students in Vegas. None of them are fucking wimps.'" For the most part this is in John's notes, and it's along the same lines as other things Hickey has said: for example, in the book *New Hotel Design* by Otto Riewoldt, Hickey is quoted as saying that Las Vegas is "the only authentic image-world on the North American continent."

"I wanted to leave my mark on this city," casino owner Bob Stupak once said about his Stratosphere, the tallest American building west of the Mississippi. "What I wanted to do for Vegas is what the Eiffel Tower did for Paris, or what the Empire State Building did for New York . . . I wanted my building to be a symbol, to be synonymous with Vegas itself."

"Indeed," said Dave Hickey, an art critic at the University of Nevada in Las Vegas. "He definitely created a new symbol for Las Vegas. But that still begs the question: What does the symbol mean?"

Dave Hickey has been called the city's resident art historian, an ambassador for Las Vegas to the rest of the world.

"You know why I like it here?" he said. "Because everything in this city is economically driven. And that's the only true democracy there is in this country. That's why I like teaching art students in Vegas. None of them are fucking wimps."

"... the Fireside Lounge, a room of red couches, octagonal tables, a neon strip of blue surrounding pit fires, and mirrors on every wall, floor-to-ceiling, wall-to-wall." OK, now he calls it a lounge. The essay got it right even if the notes got it wrong. Anyway, the Fireside Lounge is one classy joint: voted "Best Place to Spot Showgirls" by the website *Vegas Hotspots,* and "one of the 'places to be seen'" by *Casino Magazine,* boasting the "Best Cocktail Waitress" by *Las Vegas Magazine,* and "Best Exotic Drinks and Most Romantic Bar" by *Menu Magazine.* And apparently, according to the bar's own website, it is "featured in such films as *Casino* and *Showgirls* and has been seen on TV in *CSI Las Vegas* and *Elimidate.*" (Quibble: There's no such thing as a television show called *CSI Las Vegas*; as alluded to before, the television show called *CSI: Crime Scene Investigation* takes place in Las Vegas, but they only started tagging the franchise with location names to distinguish them from the original, Vegas-located

We met one morning before nine o'clock at a bar on the Strip called the Fireside Lounge, a room of red couches, octagonal tables, a neon strip of blue surrounding pit fires, and mirrors on every wall, floor-to-ceiling, wall-to-wall.

Three men in black suits were drunk on one couch, a couple on the next was making out with loud moans, a woman on another was alone with a Bloody Mary, and Dave at the bar in black cowboy boots was funneling a free bowl of peanuts to his mouth.

"Sure," he said, "the Stratosphere's the tallest dick in Las Vegas, that's true, and when you have the biggest dick you get some respect. But I also think the fact that the building is so fucking big is why it's also had so much trouble in this town. Las Vegas architecture is about commerce, and commerce is about flexibility. There's absolutely no gap here between a thought and an act. This city prides itself on its ability to follow the whims of tourism, because that way, if something doesn't work, you're better equipped to try something else. If you build something and it fails, you just blow it up. Buildings, neighborhoods, politicians ... whatever. This city doesn't assume that anything's permanent. But

show.) But, in addition to red couches, there are also blue velvet love seats; and in addition to octagonal tables, there are also plain circular ones; and the fire pits are actually pools that have fire magically emanating from them; and while there are a lot of mirrors, they are definitely not floor-to-ceiling and wall-to-wall. That would be kind of impossible. So John should probably correct these details.

"Three men in black suits were drunk on one couch, a couple on the next was making out with loud moans, a woman on another was alone with a Bloody Mary, and Dave at the bar in black cowboy boots was funneling a free bowl of peanuts to his mouth." I saw two out of four of these things when I went to check up on the place. I think we can assume the possibility of the other stuff.

"'Sure,' he said, 'the Stratosphere's the tallest dick in Las Vegas ...' etc." Confirmed: in his notes. Also status as phallic symbol: extremely obvious.

"**In 1996, just after the Stratosphere opened its doors, experts were consulted about how it could be demolished.**" Confirmed by Ken McCall in "Tower Went Up Easier Than It Could Come Down," *Las Vegas Sun,* July 29, 1996.

"**While most buildings in Las Vegas are chicken wire, stucco, and steel support beams . . .**" Granted, there's a lot of stucco in Vegas (so much stucco . . .), but mostly you see it off the Strip. So this comparison isn't fair when pitting the place up against casinos in its own league. For instance, the Luxor is all glass, and I think the Bellagio is also solid concrete or maybe even stone or something. They aren't exactly chicken wire and stucco, in other words.

"**. . . the Stratosphere is made of several hundred thousand cubic feet of concrete.**" I'm pretty sure he's talking about the tower here, although it's a little ambiguous whether this figure includes what went into building the hotel and casino, or just the tower. I can find no exact figure on the amount of concrete used to construct it, but I can confirm that the tower as a whole weighs about a hundred million pounds—1,600 tons of which (i.e. 3.2 million pounds) is steel. The rest of it isn't all concrete, although the weight must come from somewhere. According to the website of Reade Advanced Materials, concrete is generally about 140–150 pounds per cubic foot. I guess I have no idea what the typical proportion is of concrete to steel in a tower, especially in a very concrete-heavy building like the Stratosphere, and I am also not sure what "several" means here in John's claim of "several hundred thousand." If we interpret "several" as being anywhere between three and ten, then the only useful information John's offering in his claim of "several hundred thousand cubic feet" is that it's in the range of 42 million pounds and 150 million pounds of concrete. That's pretty vague, and therefore I think it could be considered an inaccurate statement.

"**'Basically, you'd have to fell it like a giant tree,' said Mark Loizeaux . . .**" This is confirmed in the same Ken McCall article mentioned earlier in the *Las Vegas Sun,* 1996. But that article also reveals that this quote—which John is using to sound like it's an interview he conducted himself—is actually just a prettified paraphrase of what this dude said in the article. And parts of it are filled in/made up. For example, he actually said "pieces the size of your living room chair and smaller."

John: I'm not trying to make it sound like I interviewed the guy. I gave you the copy of the article that you're referring to. So I'm not hiding anything. I'm just trying to declutter the prose.

"**. . . an implosion expert who's overseen the demolition of several famous Las Vegas resorts.**" Same article as above confirms that he oversaw the implosions of the Dunes and the Landmark. Both were indeed famous hotel/casinos. Merriam-Webster says that a resort is "a place providing recreation and entertainment especially to vacationers," so I guess those were resorts—but I don't think the hotels were called such by their proprietors. For what it's worth.

---

the Stratosphere can only be exactly what it is. I mean, that thing's there to stay. And that's what's wrong with it. The Stratosphere's trapped being 'The Stratosphere' forever."

In 1996, just after the Stratosphere opened its doors, experts were consulted about how it could be demolished.

"That's a good question," said the Stratosphere's contractor.

While most buildings in Las Vegas are chicken wire, stucco, and steel support beams, the Stratosphere is made of several hundred thousand cubic feet of concrete.

"Basically, you'd have to fell it like a giant tree," said Mark Loizeaux, an implosion expert who's overseen the demolition of several famous Las Vegas resorts. "You'd incline it in one direction by tilting it explosively, and then you'd explode all the rest of it while it was falling to the ground. Basically, you'd want to turn the whole thing into gravel while it was still in midair, pieces the size of your living room couch. The biggest problem with doing that, though, is that

"In other words, an area of land on the Las Vegas Strip that was a quarter mile long, and vacant." Wrong: A mile is 5280 feet, the tower is 1149 feet, so that's .217 miles. And this isn't a direct quote from the article.

John: I was trying to make his statement a little clearer. But maybe I messed up the math.

Jim: Maybe.

"Approximately a billion dollars." The same article frames it as "The bill . . . would be more than half a billion dollars." So, not a billion, as John says, and this too isn't a direct quote.

John: All right, that was a mistake.

Jim: Score.

"'It's just not what people come to Vegas for,' said Dave." This quote is in John's notes. But I do have to say that when I first visited Las Vegas it was out of a fascination with its buildings. In fact, lots of lists online for the "top ten reasons to visit Las Vegas" mention lights and casinos, which are part of the architecture. True, none of those lists actually use the phrase "great architecture." (For what it's worth, one of those websites lists "hiring escorts to play Axis and Allies with you.")

"'Look at the most successful hotels in this town,' he said. 'What do they got in common? They're all ceilings and floors and no fucking walls.'" A building with "no fucking walls" is not strictly possible.

John: It's a quote, Jim. Leave it alone. Plus, fact-checking me is one thing, but you're frankly out of your league with Hickey. Lay off.

---

you'd need to have an area to do this in that was as wide as the building is tall."

In other words, an area of land on the Las Vegas Strip that was a quarter mile long, and vacant.

"Plus," he added, "there's the issue of cost, because you'd probably end up spending more to take this thing down than it actually cost to build."

Approximately a billion dollars.

"So I'd say it's there to stay," said Loizeaux.

"It's just not what people come to Vegas for," said Dave. "This isn't New York, this isn't Chicago, we're not a city of great buildings. We're the city of schtick and gimmick, the place that you come to when you need to escape."

From what?

"From what do you think?" said Dave.

He called a waitress over, asked for more peanuts.

"Look at the most successful hotels in this town," he said. "What do they got in common? They're all ceilings and floors and no fucking walls. Casino designers know that people don't like gambling with a lot of space above them.

"'Casino designers know that people don't like gambling with a lot of space above them.'" The book *Designing Casinos to Dominate the Competition: The Friedman International Standards of Casino Design* by Bill Friedman (now availabile in English and Japanese! Only $150!) lists a number of "principles" of Casino Design, one of which is "Principle 8: Low Ceilings Beat High Ceilings," with subsections: "Ceiling Height's Powerful Impact on Potential Play," "Ceiling Height and Player Count Interrelationships," and "The Correlation Between Ceiling Height and Competitive Ranking." The other principles are pretty interesting, including: "Principle 1: A Physically Segmented Casino Beats a Completely Open Barn"; "Principle 2: Gambling Equipment Immediately Inside Casino Entrances Beats Vacant Raised Entrance Landings and Empty Lobbies"; "Principle 3: Short Lines of Sight Beat Extensive Visible Depth"; "Principle 4: The Maze Layout Beats Long, Wide, Straight Passageways and Aisles"; "Principle 5: A Compact and Congested Gambling-Equipment Layout Beats a Vacant and Spacious Floor Layout"; "Principle 6: An Organized Gambling-Equipment Layout With Focal Points of Interest Beats a Floor Layout That Lacks a Sense of Organization"; "Principle 7: Segregated Sit-Down Facilities Beat Contiguous Ones"; "Principle 9: Gambling Equipment As the Decor Beats Impressive and Memorable Decorations"; "Principle 10: Standard Decor Beats Interior Casino Themes"; "Principle 11: Pathways Emphasizing the Gambling Equipment Beat the Yellow Brick Road"; "Principle 12: Perception

Beats Reality"; "Principle 13: Multiple Interior Settings and Gambling Ambiances Beat a Single Atmosphere Throughout." They really have everything figured out.

John: And please note Principle #12, Jim. "Perception Beats Reality."

"'So when you look at a place like the Bellagio, which is the most successful hotel this city's ever seen . . .'" A number of places mention that the Bellagio is currently the most profitable casino in Vegas. But I can't find support for this "ever seen" assertion.

"'. . . it's got this giant open floor plan of 80,000 square feet, but it's all underneath a really low ceiling. It's multilayered, if you look at it. You've got the main ceiling above everything, and then that steps down to a lower level, and then there's a hood that hangs under that, and then an awning under that. So what you end up with is a twenty-foot-high ceiling that's got nine feet of headroom.'" The casino's website actually claims 100k square feet of gambling space, but granted not all of that is in the central gambling area. It is relatively "open," however, as far as these things go (they violate some of Friedman's rules about mazes and lines of sight). Don't have the exact figures on ceiling heights, but those awnings certainly are ubiquitous.

"'Why? Because the hotel knows that the reason people come here is to be protected from God.'" Actu-

---

So when you look at a place like the Bellagio, which is the most successful hotel this city's ever seen, it's got this giant open floor plan of 80,000 square feet, but it's all underneath a really low ceiling. It's multilayered, if you look at it. You've got the main ceiling above everything, and then that steps down to a lower level, and then there's a hood that hangs under that, and then an awning under that. So what you end up with is a twenty-foot-high ceiling that's got nine feet of headroom. Why? Because the hotel knows that the reason people come here is to be protected from God. I'm serious. No one's consciously thinking about this, but that's why they're here. They want as much space between them and Jesus Christ as they can get while they're fucking around. That's why hotels that emphasize their heights don't really do well here. I mean, you've got the Luxor, right, with its light that shoots into space. That opened up in the mid-nineties as a luxury hotel, but ten years later they've got some of the lowest room rates on the Strip. Rooms at the Paris Hotel are usually discounted too, despite the fact that it cost them a billion dollars to build it. It's just not a welcoming place. It's got tons of tiny

---

ally, I think they probably do the ceiling thing because of "The Correlation between Ceiling Height and Competitive Ranking."

John: You really don't like poetry, do you?

"'That opened up in the mid-nineties as a luxury hotel, but ten years later they've got some of the lowest room rates on the Strip.'" According to a lot of travel sites, the hotel's rooms are about $125, behind only the Bellagio, Venetian, Caesars Palace, and the Four Seasons.

"'Rooms at the Paris Hotel are usually discounted too, despite the fact that it cost them a billion dollars to build it.'" Looking at the calendar, they do have discounted rates, but they seem to be seasonal, which is pretty standard. According to Frommer's, it cost $785 million to build, not $1 billion.

"'It's just not a welcoming place.'" What, he doesn't find artist-in-residence Barry Manilow a welcoming presence?

"'It's got tons of tiny windows built into its façade that create a huge towering sense of height over the viewer.'" It does, but to be fair, the Bellagio also has tons of windows built into its façade which also create "a huge towering sense of height over the viewer." Sounds like a double standard.

John: Actually, Jim, if Hickey were around to fact-check *you*, he would say that while the same amount of area on the Bellagio's façade is made up of windows, its windows are much larger than those on the façade of the Paris, since each of the Bellagio's windows actually comprise four different windows to four different rooms, and so the hotel ends up looking both less menacing and also far less "busy" when one stands before it. Hickey's right on this count.

"'No one comes to Vegas to pray.'" I'll give him this. While it's only urban legend that Vegas has more churches per capita than anywhere in America, it does in fact have more bars per capita than anywhere else.

"Initially, Bob Stupak envisioned that the Stratosphere would be the tallest sign in the world." Confirmed in that same earlier article by John Galtant, *Las Vegas Review-Journal,* October 5, 1989.

"It would stand beside the low-rise façade of his hotel, Bob Stupak's Vegas World, a twenty-story structure . . ." Ditto.

windows built into its façade that create a huge towering sense of height over the viewer. People don't want to be looking up while they're visiting this city. No one comes to Vegas to pray."

Initially, Bob Stupak envisioned that the Stratosphere would be the tallest sign in the world. It would stand beside the low-rise façade of his hotel, Bob Stupak's Vegas World, a twenty-story structure whose theme—"The Sky's the Limit"—would be written vertically in neon up the length of a rocket ship that would stand 1,000 feet high. At that time, it would have been the tenth-tallest structure on Earth.

"But around that time my daughter was living in Australia, and I went to visit her," he said. "We had lunch at the Sydney Tower, which is a thousand feet high and has a revolving restaurant at its top. I saw people standing in line for an hour just to pay for a ride in an elevator to get to its observation deck. And I suddenly had an idea. I was only trying to build a sign in Las Vegas, but what if I put an observation deck on the top of my sign? People would come from all over the country just to stand up there and look. And then at some point I asked,

". . . whose theme—'The Sky's the Limit' . . ." Ditto.

". . . written vertically in neon up the length of a rocket ship that would stand 1,000 feet high." Ditto.

"At that time, it would have been the tenth-tallest structure on Earth." Well, "structure" is certainly not true, since if you're considering all "structures," then you have to count radio towers, too, and there were of course far more than ten radio towers that were taller than the Stratosphere at that time. (And it gets really complicated if you try to dig into the terminology of "structures" vs. "towers" vs. "skyscrapers" vs. "masts.")
John: Then let's not.

"'But around that time my daughter was living in Australia, and I went to visit her,' he said." John L. Smith book again, *No Limit,* p. 143.

"... the Stratosphere Hotel has received seven awards from the *Las Vegas Review-Journal*'s annual readers' poll ..." Factual Dispute: It's actually the *Las Vegas Sun* that held an annual readers' poll, although the *Sun* has apparently now been taken over by the *Las Vegas Review-Journal,* so perhaps it's technically correct to say that the awards came from the *Las Vegas Review-Journal.*

"... 'Ugliest Las Vegas Building' ..." Confirmed: It received this honor in 1997.

"... 'Trashiest Place in Vegas' ..." Confirmed: Received this one the same year, 1997.

"... 'Hotel Most Deserving of Being Imploded' ..." Confirmed: 1997.

"... a special commendation for Bob Stupak himself: 'Most Embarrassing Thing About Las Vegas.'" Wow, I guess 1997 kind of sucked for the Stratosphere. (*No Limit: The Rise and Fall of Bob Stupak and the Stratosphere Hotel,* John L. Smith, Huntington Press, 1997, p. 198.)

"There have also been eight fires at the Stratosphere Hotel ..." I can definitely confirm at least seven of these fires, and possibly as many as nine: August 1993, during its construction ("Las Vegas News Briefs," *Las Vegas Sun,* October 30, 1999); April 26, 1996 ("Smoke, but No Towering Inferno" by Cathy Scott, *Las Vegas Sun,* April 26, 1996); July 5, 1996 ("Las Vegas News Briefs," *Las Vegas Sun,* July 5, 1996); April 16, 1997 ("Wastebasket Fire Leads to Evacuation at Stratosphere," *Las Vegas Sun,* April 16, 1997); March 2000 (*Fire Engineering* 153, no. 3 [March 2000]: 46, although in this article it's stated that "a fire accidentally started by a candle on the second floor of the Bath and Body Works retail store in the Stratosphere Hotel and Casino in Las Vegas, Nevada, was put out by the sprinkler system even before the firefighters arrived," so it was a pretty weak "fire"); January 13, 2003 ("News Briefs for January 13, 2003: Sprinklers Douse Stratosphere Fire," *Las Vegas Sun,* January 13, 2003); and September 3, 2005 ("Traffic, Lake Deaths Mar Weekend" by Mary Manning, *Las Vegas Sun,* September 6, 2005).

"... one of which broke out during its opening celebration." Factual Dispute: This "fire," which broke out on April 29, 1996 (as reported in "Smoke Strands Guests Atop Tower," *Sun* Staff, *Las Vegas Sun,* May 1, 1996), was not actually a fire, but rather just a lot of smoke from a fireworks display that went awry and set off the fire alarms.

"There has been one guest strangled to death in his hotel room by strangers ..." Confirmed in "Court Briefs for October 9, 2001," *Las Vegas Sun,* October 9, 2001.

"... a machine gun fired in its parking garage ..." Confirmed in "Police Defend Coverage of Violence-Prone Area," *Las Vegas Sun,* March 12, 1997.

"... and a lawsuit involving over 18,000 plaintiffs." Confirmed: It was a class-action lawsuit filed on behalf of almost 19,000 defaulted vacation packages: "Though Stupak raised more than $25 million

'Well, why can't it go higher?' Which is when I decided to make the sign 1,149 feet high, instead of just 1,000 feet high, because that seemed like a more scientific number. And then that's when the whole idea of building the world's tallest sign stopped being our main concern, because we realized that that's what we were already doing. The very structure itself would be an advertisement."

Since 1996, the Stratosphere Hotel has received seven awards from the *Las Vegas Review-Journal*'s annual readers' poll, including "Ugliest Las Vegas Building," "Trashiest Place in Vegas," "Hotel Most Deserving of Being Imploded," and a special commendation for Bob Stupak himself: "Most Embarrassing Thing About Las Vegas."

There have also been eight fires at the Stratosphere Hotel, three of which occurred before the hotel even opened, and one of which broke out during its opening celebration.

There has been one guest strangled to death in his hotel room by strangers, a machine gun fired in its parking garage, and a lawsuit involving over 18,000 plaintiffs.

by selling nineteen thousand vacation packages, he ran out of money and was forced to cede control of Stratosphere to Grand. In January 1997, faced with the realization that the $4.4 million in cash and stock in Stupak's escrow account was not nearly enough to cover the $15 million in vacation obligations, Stratosphere said it would no longer honor the packages. The package-holders subsequently sued Stupak and Stratosphere, which declared bankruptcy in early 1997. That suit was granted class-action status last June" ("Stratosphere to Honor Stupak's Vacation Packages" by John Wilen, *Las Vegas Sun,* April 6, 1998). Oops, their bad.

means that regulations would start at 412 feet. But, the FAA only concerns itself with buildings over 781 feet tall. That suggests that there is a range of about 412 feet to 781 feet that are over airport regulation but which the FAA doesn't care about.

John: Are you purposefully trying to complicate this? What does it matter? I've got a source for the information, which is all that you seem to care about. That, and apparently whistle-blowing on federal agencies.

"There was the Federal Aviation Administration's warning that the architect's plan for the 1,000-foot-high tower was 600 feet over airport regulations." Factual Dispute: The FAA concerns itself with any building that is over 781 feet high, and so they were worried in 1991 that Stupak's tower (which was then proposed at 1,012 feet) would create a "substantial adverse impact" on flight patterns. So it seems unlikely that the original proposal for the structure was 600 feet over regulations if it was only c. 230 feet over the minimum height the FAA deals with, right? (*No Limit: The Rise and Fall of Bob Stupak,* John L. Smith, Huntington Press, 1997, p. 198.) John, source for this?

There was the Federal Aviation Administration's warning that the architect's plan for the 1,000-foot-high tower was 600 feet over airport regulations. And then there was the response from the mayor of Las Vegas that "it's [the FAA's] job to make planes safe for Vegas, it's not the other way around."

There was, for a long time, when construction on it began, the rumor of an anomaly that locals called a "kink," a bend in one of the tower's three 800-foot-high legs, which the Stratosphere's contractor assured city residents was not a significant structural defect, but which some months later, on an early desert morning, disappeared after it was spray-filled with Styrofoam and painted.

"And then there was the response from the mayor of Las Vegas that 'it's [the FAA's] job to make planes safe for Vegas, it's not the other way around.'" According to "Consultant Calls Tower Obstacle to Air Traffic," *Las Vegas Sun,* June 3, 1994.

"There was, for a long time, when construction on it began, the rumor of an anomaly that locals called a 'kink,' a bend in one of the tower's three 800-foot-high legs, which the Stratosphere's contractor assured city residents was not a significant structural defect, but which some months later, on an early desert morning, disappeared after it was spray-filled with Styrofoam and painted." I can't find evidence of this. John?

John: Your logic here doesn't work. You think that a tower that's 600 feet over FAA regulations would be too overwhelming for them to deal with? That if something were a manageable height, then they would definitely go after the builders, but if it's a lot higher than that they're more likely to say "Fuck it, we're too overwhelmed by its height"?

Jim: That's not what I'm saying . . . What I'm saying is that if the originally proposed tower height of 1,012 feet was 600 feet over the FAA's regulations, then this

John: The "rumor" about the Stratosphere kink is entirely anecdotal, which is why it's called a "rumor." I took my first trip to Las Vegas in the summer of 1994, during which time the tower was still under construction. On a bus tour I took from Las Vegas to Hoover Dam, we sat briefly in traffic at the foot of the tower, and the bus driver— who doubled as our tour guide—told us that one of the three legs on the tower's tripod was crooked and that because the sight of it so unnerved local residents (even though it was supposedly safe) the building's contractor filled in the leg's crooked angle with Styrofoam.

Jim: Hmm . . . do you have any documentation of that, like notes from your trip?

John: You're asking me for evidence of a rumor?

Jim: If you're saying that there was a rumor, I have to find out if there was in fact a rumor, even if I ignore the truth value of the rumor. Do you remember the name of the company that ran the tour?

John: Are you serious?

Jim: It would be pretty late in the game to start joking now.

John: No, I don't remember the name of a tour company from more than fifteen years ago. Sorry, readers are going to have to feel factually unfulfilled here.

Jim: Then what about the notes you took during that trip?

John: In 1994 I was a sophomore in college, studying Latin and Greek—not writing—and on vacation with my grandparents. We were going to Hoover Dam on a thousand-hour-long bus trip through the desert without any air-conditioning. No notes were being taken, Jim.

Bankruptcy" by Adam Steinhauer, *Las Vegas Review-Journal,* January 28, 1997.

John: It's been abbreviated to "$500 million" for the sake of rhythm.

". . . and the $800 million that it accumulated in debt." Factual Dispute: Should be $887 million, not "$800 million," according to "Stratosphere Creditors Coming Out of the Woodwork" by Brian Seals, *Las Vegas Sun,* May 1, 1998.

John: Rhythm.

There was, before its opening, the hotel's stock price of $14.

And then, once it opened, its price of 2¢.

There was the $35 million it was supposed to cost to build, the $500 million it actually cost to build, and the $800 million it accumulated in debt.

There was the hotel's bankruptcy.

There was the man from Utah who jumped off in 2000.

The man from Britain who jumped off after that.

The jump by the producer of *Las Vegas Elvis,* a local reality television show about one of the city's official Elvis Presley impersonators, who said to reporters, when he heard of the jump, "Now whenever I see it, the Stratosphere is going to be my heartbreak hotel."

"There was, before its opening, the hotel's stock price of $14." Confirmed in "Stratosphere to Honor Stupak's Vacation Packages," John Wilen, *Las Vegas Sun,* April 6, 1998.

"There was the hotel's bankruptcy." Confirmed: "Stratosphere Stock Mystery Explained" by Gary Thompson, *Las Vegas Sun,* February 26, 1998.

"There was the man from Utah who jumped off in 2000." Confirmed: "Man Jumps to Death from the Top of 1,149-foot Hotel-Casino Tower," by Trevor Hayes, *Las Vegas Journal-Review,* January 6, 2000.

"The man from Britain who jumped off after that." Confirmed: "Man Jumps from Stratosphere Tower," *Las Vegas Review-Journal,* February 8, 2006.

"The jump by the producer of *Las Vegas Elvis,* a local reality television show about one of the city's official Elvis Presley impersonators, who said to reporters, when he heard of the jump, 'Now whenever I see it, the Stratosphere is going to be my heartbreak hotel.'" Factual Disputes: Proper title of that reality show was *Vegas Elvis* ("Tragedy Follows *Elvis* Show Work," *Las Vegas Review-Journal,* March 30, 2005). I also have found nothing to confirm that this man is an "official Elvis Presley impersonator." And a correction is needed in the quote: "Melanie was a beautiful person and now to me the Stratosphere will always be a Heart Break

"And then, once it opened, its price of 2¢." Confirmed: "Stratosphere Stock Mystery Explained" by Gary Thompson, *Las Vegas Sun,* February 26, 1998.

"There was the $35 million it was supposed to cost to build . . ." Confirmed, *No Limit,* p. 171.

". . . the $500 million that it actually cost to build . . ." Factual Dispute: This "$500 million" should actually be $550 million, according to "Stratosphere Files

Hotel" ("Heartbreak Hits *Vegas Elvis* Reality Show," *Casino City Times,* April 13 2005).

John: The sentence sounds better as I've reworked it. And I haven't changed the gist of what he's saying.

"**. . . alone in the sky . . .**" Factual Dispute: The Stratosphere is by no means "alone in the sky" in Vegas. There are tons of other tall buildings going up every day. Certainly it is the tallest, that's true, and by far it's the highest in that part of the city. But the Stratosphere definitely isn't "alone in the sky." John's exaggerating.

John: I meant emotionally "alone"—meaning that the building is sad and lonely-looking, despite being surrounded by other buildings. You have to allow for a bit of poetry, Jim. Although I also maintain that there is some physical truth to this, because the tower was essentially alone in the sky at the time of Levi's death. The recent burst of construction in Las Vegas has added a lot of high-rises to the skyline, but for a long time the Stratosphere was indeed "alone" over the city.

"**. . . nursing home window: alone in the sky . . .**" Ditto. But I can confirm that there are a good number of nursing, convalescent, and retirement homes in Vegas that theoretically one could look out the windows of.

"**And when coming into the city on 95 from the north or 15 from the south or 93 from the east, there are the 5 or the 16 or the 21 miles during which the Stratosphere stands alone in the distance . . .**" Factual Dispute: Sounds like this was written from memory without any use of a map. While Highway 15 does come in from the south, it would be more accurate to say that Highway 95 comes from the northwest and Highway 93 comes from the northeast. But in fact, both seem to come into the city at comparable angles. And if you are approaching the city from the south, the tower doesn't really appear to stand alone in the distance. From the airport (which is to the south of the Strip), I had to look around for it because it was blocked out by the palm trees that were near me, and once I did find it, only the needle of the tower stuck up above the mountains. When I asked people working at the airport if they could point the tower out to me, they had to look around for a while to find it. So it's not like it's a local landmark that's indelibly present in the consciousness of all Las Vegans or anything. (I wonder how many Las Vegans are vegans? Visions of cruelty-free showgirl wardrobes abound.) Luckily, however, there are people out there dedicated to photographing the city at every major interval along each of these highways. So, assuming from the parallel structure of John's prose that the statements being made are that "the Stratosphere stands alone in the distance for 5 miles on 95 from the north," "the Stratosphere stands alone in the distance for 16 miles on 15 from the south," and "the Stratosphere stands alone in the distance for 21 miles on 93 from the east," I checked out photographs on *RockyMountain Roads.com* to determine if these claims are accurate. From the north on the 95 at the 5-mile mark the tallest things you can see are just streetlights and power lines near the road; not the tower. From the south on the 15, the tower is visible, but so are a lot of other casinos. And from the east/north on the 93, there are only pictures from where the 93 merges with the 15, and at that point you're still in the mountains, which are all you see.

"**. . . the valley's high rim of black mountains . . .**" Dispute: The mountains around Las Vegas vary in color throughout the day. In some areas they look brown and in others they look black, and then at other times they look bright orange. From my observation, the mountains to the east are brownish in appearance. The ones that look black are to the southeast.

"**. . . alone at the middle of the Las Vegas Strip, alone at the end of a bridge called Poets Bridge, a few blocks from the tower . . .**" Factual Dispute: First of

> There is its appearance from a schoolyard trampoline: alone in the sky on the long brown horizon.
>
> There is its appearance from a nursing home window: alone in the sky above the treeline.
>
> And when coming into the city on 95 from the north or 15 from the south or 93 from the east, there are the 5 or the 16 or the 21 miles during which the Stratosphere stands alone in the distance, alone over the valley's high rim of black mountains, alone at the middle of the Las Vegas Strip, alone at the end

all, the bridge John's talking about is located at Lewis Avenue and 14th Street, neither of which is considered "the Strip." And while this intersection is roughly parallel to what would be considered the "middle" of the Las Vegas Strip, it would nevertheless be inaccurate to claim that this bridge is located on the Strip. Second of all, what exactly is it that John is claiming is "at the end of a bridge called Poets Bridge"? Isn't a bridge, by definition, open-ended? Which end is he talking about? Which side are we starting from? Where are we? John's syntax is wildly confusing here, or perhaps it's intentionally vague because he knows that he's BS-ing these figures. And third of all, this intersection is almost two miles away from the Stratosphere. According to an estimate I found online, the average city block in the American Southwest is about 0.1 mile long, so two miles in Las Vegas would roughly equal 15–20 city blocks. This hardly qualifies as "a few blocks."

John: I'm building an image, Jim.

Jim: An image based on what? Your imagination?

John: An image based on a certain sense of the city that I am not alone in feeling. The Stratosphere and the Poets Bridge are in the same general Las Vegas neighborhood, which is the technical point here. But the more important point is that they both contribute to the emotional ambience of the city that I happen to feel while I'm there, and this image—as I'm constructing it—is meant to provide the reader with a sense of that ambience.

Jim: But if you're constructing that "ambience" out of complete fabrications, then all you're really doing is imposing your own subjective feelings on an entire city. That's not very responsible.

John: I am not the first person to suggest that Las Vegas is a sad place, Jim.

". . . in a rough part of town . . ." Factual Dispute: According to the *Insider's Guide to Las Vegas* (3rd Edition), downtown Las Vegas, where this bridge is located, is full of lawyers, government buildings, and sandwich shops: "The downtown area, covering a two-mile radius emanating from Fremont Street and Las Vegas Boulevard, has long been a center for courts, banks, government and, of course, casinos. On the edge of downtown is the Gateway District. This area is emerging as an arts district, with the Arts Factory on Charleston Boulevard as its cultural hub. A converted warehouse, the Factory houses an array of arts organizations and businesses." So this doesn't seem to fit John's description of "a rough part of town." According to the *Insider's Guide,* the "rough parts" of town are in the west and south-central sections of the city, which, as the *Insider* puts it, "have the look of mean streets."

of a bridge called Poets Bridge, a few blocks from the tower, in a rough part of town, upon which someone has written with black magic marker—over the concrete verses that are inscribed on the bridge—*You wonder what you'll do when you reach the edge of the map, out there on the horizon, all that neon beckoning you in from the dark.*

". . . upon which someone has written with black magic marker—over the concrete verses that are inscribed on the bridge— *You wonder what you'll do when you reach the edge of the map, out there on the horizon, all that neon beckoning you in from the dark."* Factual Dispute: These lines are actually among those inscribed right into the concrete of the bridge, not written on it. There's actually nothing written in black magic marker anywhere on the bridge, nor any vandalism of any kind that I saw. Seems like John was trying to inflate these lines with some mysterious significance by suggesting that they were impulsively scrawled onto the bridge by a rebellious teenager or something, rather than chosen (probably by a committee commissioned by a bureaucratic state agency) to provide the city with mediocre public art. The fact is, though, that the lines are cited (right there on the concrete), and come from a guy named Kirk Robertson, who looks like he's written about twenty books of poetry and even appears on the University of Nevada at Reno's "Nevada Writers Hall of Fame." So this isn't really the "anti-establishment" vibe John was trying to create, unfortunately. Sorry to ruin it.

John: OK, I may have imagined the magic marker.

7

"After that first evening on the suicide hotline, I called around to find out who Levi Presley was." This is merely personal anecdote, and not in John's notes. I should also note that this whole "first evening" thing sounds particularly suspicious.

John: Why?

"I tried to call his parents, but their number wasn't listed." As previously mentioned, I determined that it would not be worth the effort to find a contemporaneous phone book. However, a simple Internet search easily brings up their phone number and address. If they're the type of folks who make the effort to remove their name from the phone book, I can't imagine they'd choose to let it be easily available online. It's a pretty simple process to get your personal info deleted from those websites. So this too I'm suspicious of.

"I tried to go to his funeral, but his service wasn't public." Confirmed, sort of. The death notice for Levi Presley in the *Las Vegas Review-Journal* lists the funeral home handling Levi's ceremony as "Affordable Cremation and Burial Service." I phoned their office, and while they didn't have records on hand of Levi's funeral specifically, they did confirm that pretty much all of the funeral services they do are informally limited to just family and close friends. (They don't turn people away at the door, but they don't particularly publicize or give out information about who is being buried when randoms like John call in.)

After that first evening on the suicide hotline, I called around to find out who Levi Presley was.

I tried to call his parents, but their number wasn't listed.

I tried to go to his funeral, but his service wasn't public.

I even called an ad that I had found in the yellow pages: *Venus Investigations*—a private investigation firm for "unusual and difficult cases."

Venus had a smoker's voice, a barking dog and screaming kids and *Jeopardy!* on in the background.

Four hundred dollars' cash, she said. For "vital information."

I sent the money wired.

Five days later Venus called with Levi's middle name. Told me Levi's parents had first met in Arizona. Told me Levi hadn't ever committed any crimes. Told me where they lived, and then she said, "And there's a tape."

"A tape?" I asked.

"A security tape."

Every incident in a hotel in the city of Las Vegas is recorded by thousands of cameras that are embedded in the ceilings.

". . . a private investigation firm for 'unusual and difficult cases.'" Factual Dispute: A photocopy John provided of this ad reads "Specializing in Unusual and Difficult Cases."

"Venus had a smoker's voice, a barking dog and screaming kids and *Jeopardy!* on in the background." These Venus details are in John's notes. *Jeopardy!* is spelled correctly. I can't believe Alex Trebek shaved his 'stache, that's such a loss.

"Four hundred dollars' cash, she said. For 'vital information.' I sent the money wired." I can actually confirm this with a receipt John included with his material. It indicates that a wire transfer of $400 was sent by John to—lo and behold!—one Ms. Venus Lovetere of Las Vegas, Nevada.

"Five days later Venus called with Levi's middle name. Told me Levi's parents had first met in Arizona. Told me Levi hadn't ever committed any crimes. Told me where they lived . . ." Personal anecdote, and not in his notes.

"'And there's a tape.'" Confirmed: There is reference in the Coroner's Report of Levi being recorded at the Stratosphere prior to his suicide.

"Every incident in a hotel in the city of Las Vegas is recorded by thousands of cameras that are embedded in the ceilings." Factual Dispute: It is an illegal invasion of privacy to have cameras in an area in which someone might be "expectant of privacy"—i.e., in bathrooms, spas, or hotel rooms (according to an article on "Electronic Monitoring in the Workplace: Common Law & Federal Statutory Protection"). So, technically speaking, not "every incident in a Las Vegas hotel" is recorded.

"Levi liked going to Applebee's. In-N-Out. A place that's now out of business, [etc.]" Continuity Quibble: Even ignoring whether or not each of these things is true, the list doesn't match up precisely with the original one that John offered concerning Levi: "What I know for certain about Levi Presley is what he looked like, how old he was, what kind of car he drove, what school he attended, what girl he liked and what girl liked him, his favorite outfit, favorite movie, favorite restaurant, favorite band, what level belt he held in Tae Kwon Do, what design he had sketched onto the wall of his bedroom—very lightly, in pencil—and later planned to fill in, which drawings of his from art school he is thought to have been particularly proud of and

"So if someone's cheating at cards," Venus said over the phone, "or if there's a fight somewhere, a murder, any kind of shit, the hotel can edit together all the relevant footage and send it to the Vegas police. It limits their liability."

"And they made one of these of Levi?"

"That's what I'm hearing, man. Yeah."

"I wonder if I could see it."

"Now why the fuck would you want that?"

Levi liked going to Applebee's.

In-N-Out.

A place that's now out of business.

He wore a lot of white.

Sometimes a silver chain.

And purple-tinted glasses.

He liked a girl named Mary.

Also Eminem.

Was called by his mom "my little booper."

His Chrysler LeBaron was "Goose."

He said that he was sad.

I asked about what.

quiz he took in school—*What is good? What is bad? What does 'art' mean to you? Now look at the chair on the table in front of you and describe it in literal terms*—and of which bottle of cologne among the five Levi kept in the medicine cabinet down the hall his small bedroom still smelled, even after his parents had ripped up its carpeting, thrown out its bed, and emptied its closet of everything but his art, by the time I first visited them, three months after his death." So that's pretty sloppy, especially considering John's obsession with the "artistic effects" of things. I mean, shouldn't this catalogue be reordered to match the original?

John: No. This version of the list is designed to gradually move from information about Levi that is not particularly intimate (like his favorite restaurant) toward that which we might consider very intimate (like his mom's nickname for him, or what I thought he and I talked about on the phone).

"He said that he was sad. I asked about what. He said some stuff. I asked like what. Doesn't matter. Why not. Just sucks. Hung up." There is no evidence of this exchange in John's notes, other than the reference in his hotline counselor's journal that someone "young" called and then

whether their themes could be said to provide an indication of suicidal 'ideation,' the nickname of his car, the two different nicknames his parents had each given him, his answers to the questions on the last pop

eventually "hung up." And, as I mentioned earlier, it seems odd that John would be able to remember verbatim this conversation, especially if, as he says in the piece, he initially dismissed this kid's call. It's all just very fishy, and not the Swedish kind.

"I sat beside the Presleys on a green leather La-Z-Boy sectional recliner with the ceramic black urn of Levi's ashes in my lap." La-Z-Boy spelling confirmed. There's no mention of Levi's cremation in the paper, nor of the ceramic black urn in John's notes, but the aforementioned funeral home was called "Affordable Cremation and Burial Service," so perhaps it's safe to take John at his word on this. I can also confirm that it's common that urns be ceramic.

"We were beneath their cathedral ceiling. We were watching TV Land. We had nuts and we had Triscuits and we had spinach dip and Coke. We ate soup and then a salad and then chicken and then brownies. We looked for several minutes at his art in their new den." Apparently a "cathedral ceiling" is just an ordinary ceiling that slopes and is attached to the roof or something. Sources also note that such ceilings are difficult to insulate, but the Presleys do live in the desert, so perhaps this isn't a concern. Most of these details are not in John's notes, however. But there are some references to Levi's artwork. Spelling of TV Land confirmed on the TV Land website.

John: A ceiling that is "attached to the roof or something"? This is your idea of rigorous fact-checking?

"We drove across the valley to Tae Kwon Do for Kids . . ." According to John's notes, the actual name of this Tae Kwon Do studio is "Cory Martin's ATA Black Belt Academy and Karate for Kids." So where the heck John got this name from is a mystery, as is why he decided to change it.

John: I did it for the sake of simplification. What Levi studied at Cory's studio was Tae Kwon Do, and yet the studio's name would suggest that someone wouldn't be able to study Tae Kwon Do there. So, in order to avoid any unnecessary confusion—and in order to avoid a complicated and clunky explanation that detailed how Levi would have been able to study Tae Kwon Do at a Karate studio—I changed the name. And the world has not ended!

". . . and coached others after school." Confirmed: According to John's notes, Levi's mother says he was helping train some young kids at the studio after school.

"In his studies, the ancient Indian prince who invented Tae Kwon Do . . ." Factual Dispute: According to the American Tae Kwon Do Association's website, and confirmed by a wide array of many other sources, Tae Kwon Do wasn't developed until the 1950s, so it is unlikely that anyone who could be considered "ancient" invented it. In addition, the American Tae Kwon Do Association traces the form's origin to a style called "t'aekyon," which was developed in Korea, not India: "Although its roots can be somewhat traced back to antiquity, it is a historic fact that Tae Kwon Do as an organized art is relatively modern. In fact, its only documented history begins in Korea in the mid-1900s . . . although the actual form of Tae Kwon Do wasn't official until 1955 when a Korean General named Hong Hi Choi organized a movement to unify his country's various martial arts styles in a

---

He said some stuff.

I asked like what.

Doesn't matter.

Why not.

Just sucks.

Hung up.

I sat beside the Presleys on a green leather La-Z-Boy sectional recliner with the ceramic black urn of Levi's ashes in my lap.

We were beneath their cathedral ceiling.

We were watching TV Land.

We had nuts and we had Triscuits and we had spinach dip and Coke.

We ate soup and then a salad and then chicken and then brownies.

We looked for several minutes at his art in their new den.

We drove across the valley to Tae Kwon Do for Kids, the studio Levi practiced at and coached others after school.

In his studies, the ancient Indian prince who invented Tae Kwon Do

single practice. He presented the name 'Tae Kwon Do' to a committee specially formed to select a name for the new art. On April 11, 1955, Tae Kwon Do was recognized as the name for the newly unified and officially recognized Korean martial art." All I can find that supports John's theory that Tae Kwon Do originated in India is a link to a unrepentantly Geocities-esque website that describes an Indian Prince as the potential inventor of Karate (but not Tae Kwon Do): "It is generally accepted that Karate had its beginnings in India around 450 A.D. Oral tradition tells us of a wealthy Indian Prince who experimented with slaves by jabbing them with needles to find the weak parts of the body. He also watched animals as they fought. He noticed how, for instance, the Tiger tensed its body before spinning into action and how it used its claws to tear its opponent. He also watched the movements of other animals and adapted them to the human body. Having done this, he experimented on his slaves, this time using actual punches and kicks instead of needles to discover where and how to strike his opponent in order to achieve the desired effect. According to the legend, over 100 slaves were killed in this bizarre experiment." So, putting aside the fact that what the website is dubiously describing is a history of Karate (again, not Tae Kwon Do), it also goes on to disclaim the accuracy of the very story it's presenting: "This document is partially based upon spoken tradition, and the accuracy of this document depends upon the accuracy of those traditions." It's admitting, in other words, that what it's proffering is hearsay. John, any more solid sources?

John: It's not "hearsay;" it's legend. There's a difference. Oral histories are just as legitimate as other kinds of history; in fact, I'd say they're even more trustworthy because they are formed organically rather than institutionally.

Jim: Well, that's certainly a can of worms that we could go into, but I'll avoid it for the sake of my own sanity. In this case, what I would draw your attention to is the fact that in a different section of this same website the standard origin of Tae Kwon Do is also offered, thus completely contradicting the story of your dear Indian prince: "Tae Kwon Do is the Korean term for a system of unarmed combat that is virtually identical to Japanese Karate, and indeed was influenced in recent times by Japanese Karate. The origins of Tae Kwon Do, however, can be traced to ancient Korean history. Chuan Fa was introduced into northern Korea by Buddhist monks during the 4th century, and evolved into a form called Tae Kyon. The skills eventually spread beyond the temples and were passed on as a system of self-protection. Religious statues from the Silla period (A.D. 668–935) depict Karate-like techniques, suggesting a close association between Tae Kyon and religion at the time." How "trustworthy" is a website that changes its story paragraph-to-paragraph?

John: You're missing the point.

Jim: Enlighten me.

John: The point is that this website—while admittedly kind of sloppy structurally—is trying to suggest that (1) the origins of Tae Kwon Do are in Karate, that (2) it's possible that the origins of Karate are in India, and (3) that all of these histories are questionable. So it's attributing this history to legend. And where I come from, in the world of "literary nonfiction"—which is to say the world of essay-as-literature as opposed to essay-as-explanation—it isn't necessary, nor even appropriate, to demand the same kind of rigorous accuracy from a legend as we would from a fact.

Jim: But you're not attributing this to legend, nor are you citing your sources as legends. You're presenting this as fact. And I, the hypothetical reader, am putting my trust in you to give me the straight dope, or at least to make some effort to warn me whenever you're saying something that is patently untrue, even if it's untrue for "artistic reasons." I mean, what exactly gives you the authority to introduce half-baked legend as fact and sidestep questions of facticity?

John: It's called art, dickhead.

Jim: That's your excuse for everything.

John: It's not an "excuse," Jim, it's how I approach the genre. In that paragraph, I'm introducing a 1,600-year-old history from India about a guy who supposedly developed a technique for battling his enemies by sticking needles into his slaves and noting the degrees of pain he produced. It's ridiculous on its surface. Don't you think that the average reader is going to recognize that and take this all with a grain of salt?

> thrust long silver needles into the bodies of his slaves, systematically mapping their most vulnerable parts. Gradually, throughout his life, the prince learned that some thrusts could cause unbearable pain, that others caused paralysis, and that sometimes with the right thrust the prince could kill a slave.

Jim: But if you think it's "ridiculous" and if you're assuming that the reader will "take this all with a grain of salt," then why not caveat it? It's fake history, and it's misleading.

John: Because it's a cool story. It's a lot more interesting than a story about a committee in the 1950s creating Tae Kwon Do because some Communist general thought that there were too many forms of martial arts and wanted to streamline hundreds of years' worth of Korean traditions. The story about the Indian prince is evocative; it casts a more intriguing atmosphere around Tae Kwon Do. And since taking part in a Tae Kwon Do tournament was the last thing Levi did before he died, I'd like to give the sport some significance, and I'd also like it to have more resonance in the essay. The story of the Indian prince gives Tae Kwon Do that resonance, more so than a Communist committee meeting.

Jim: I understand that art without resonance is boring. But this is a place where you're inventing "significance." It's not like you're interpreting empirical data and prophetically unveiling to us a meaning that was hiding there all along. You're threading Levi's life through a needle that you're constructing.

John: As long as that story about the Indian prince is believed by *somebody*, then I consider it a legitimate potential history, and not an invention. It's an idea about Tae Kwon Do that exists in the world, and so that's how I'm choosing to frame this part of Levi's life. For all we know, it could be how Levi preferred to interpret Tae Kwon Do as well.

Jim: Oh Jesus. John, I'm all for postmodernism, and the varieties of interpretation that can shape how we approach the past, but I think it's also undeniable that there is actually an objective past made up of real actions and real statements from real people in the world, however clumsy or inaccurate we are at recording it or approximating it or making meaning out of it in our mental models. One of the purposes of history, other than interpreting and making meaning out of the past, is to figure out what in fact actually happened. Among the many attempts at constructing this record, some are more objectively valid than others. But you seem to be implying that this is arbitrary, that what a half-baked website says is equally valid as a well-recorded fact with a preponderance of evidence backing it up. I agree that we should be open to new interpretations of history, but just because you're open to new interpretations doesn't mean that all interpretations are valid. And in this case, there is a much more valid history available that you are choosing to ignore just to suit your literary needs. And that would be fine, if you were presenting this as fiction, but you're not presenting this as fiction. You're presenting this as history.

John: Jim, have you ever stopped to consider that maybe those aren't the only two options available? That maybe there is a third (or even a fourth or fifth or sixth) alternative? That our understanding of the world can't be categorized into either "fictional" or "historical" slots—with nothing in between? We all believe in emotional truths that could never hold water, but we still cling to them and insist on their relevance.

Jim: If I have to start fact-checking emotional truths, I'm getting a different job.

John: Great. I'll write you a recommendation.

> "But Tae Kwon Do isn't about killing," said Levi's coach. "It's about possessing the knowledge to do something and then restraining yourself from it."
>
> We were sitting in his office among piles of trophy pieces, helping the coach prepare for a tournament the next day by screwing tiny kickers into braided sequined pillars and then dark wooden bases that read *ACHIEVEMENT* on their plaques.

"'But Tae Kwon Do isn't about killing,' said Levi's coach. 'It's about possessing the knowledge to do something and then restraining yourself from it.'" There's evidence that John spoke with Cory Martin while visiting his studio with Levi's parents. But none of this conversation is actually recorded in his notes.

"We were sitting in his office among piles of trophy pieces, helping the coach prepare for a tournament the next day by screwing tiny kickers into braided sequined pillars and then dark wooden bases that read *ACHIEVEMENT* on their plaques." All I've got in John's notes about this trophy-assembling stuff is the exclamation "TROPHIES!" I guess we could "interpret" that as helping put together trophies, especially since free-form "interpretation" seems to overrule everything now.

"I learned that Tae Kwon Do only has nine levels . . ." He learned wrong. There are actually eleven colored levels to Tae Kwon Do: white, orange, yellow, camouflage, green, purple, blue, brown, red, red/black, and then black (source: American Tae Kwon Do website). But also, according to Encarta, "the ranking system in Tae Kwon Do is divided into ten *kup* or pupil levels." So there is no evidence of Tae Kwon Do making use of the mystical significance of the number nine, as John seems to hope it would. I realize that this is problematic, given the fact that the entire structure of John's essay is based on this misinformation, but I can't change the facts (unlike John . . .). And not to twist the knife, but it seems that if there is any one number with "significance" in Tae Kwon Do, it's the number eight, not nine: "The World Tae Kwon Do Federation . . . recognizes two basic approaches to teaching Tae Kwon Do, each of which is made up of eight sets. Both of these sets of eight are based on the ancient text the *Book of Changes,* or *I Ching,* in which eight different combinations of Um Yang/Yin Yang are defined . . . The eight stages are: Heaven, Joyfulness, Fire, Thunder, Wind, Water, Mountains, and Earth."

John: I got this from Levi's coach. So if this is how Levi was taught Tae Kwon Do, then this is how I'm going to present it.

". . . and then a whole separate series of advanced black belts, each with its own complexity of reticulated levels, nine tiers of nine grades in nine stages

without end . . ." This is almost right. According to Wikipedia—which would qualify in John's world as a "potentially valid non-institutional oral history"— "The reason for nine black belt degrees, according to General Choi, is that the number nine is not only the highest of the single-digit numbers, but that it is also the number of three multiplied by three. In the Orient, three is the most esteemed of all numbers." So, at least they acknowledge John's claim that there are nine different stages within the black belt. But this business about "nine tiers of nine grades in nine stages without end" is nowhere in sight, and I doubt it exists anywhere other than in John's precious imagination. You've got to ask yourself how far on the fringes of facticity someone is if not even Wikipedia agrees with them.

". . . because Korean culture does not believe we can be perfect." This seems like a peculiarly romanticized interpretation of an entire culture. What's the source for this, John?

John: I really don't care at this point. You're being an ass.

Jim: But where'd you get this from?

John: I'm not participating in this process any longer.

"I think because it's thought that Levi fell for nine seconds." Once again, according to the coroner, as well as the hotel's recording of Levi's death, his fall off the tower only lasted eight seconds.

I learned that Tae Kwon Do only has nine levels—there is white, yellow, orange, green, blue, purple, red, and brown, and then a whole separate series of advanced black belts, each with its own complexity of reticulated levels, nine tiers of nine grades in nine stages without end—because Korean culture does not believe we can be perfect.

Then someone said "Hmm" as he finished up another trophy.

I think because it's thought that Levi fell for nine seconds.

When you multiply a holy number to itself, such as three, you get a sacred number.

I learned, for example, that the ninth order of heaven is where God himself resides.

That before he could receive the secret meaning of runes, Odin had to hang for nine days on a tree.

That there are always nine Muses alive at any time.

Always nine Maidens in ancient Celtic myths.

Always nine floors in the most sacred Buddhist temples.

If a servant finds nine peas in a pod and places that pod on the floor of her kitchen, the first man who comes in and tramples that pod will be the man she marries.

Nine knots in a string of wool will cure a broken ankle.

"When you multiply a holy number to itself, such as three, you get a sacred number." Factual Dispute: I honestly have no idea what this means, nor where it comes from. And John has no evidence of investigating this in his notes. It's true that in a variety of religious traditions the number three is considered mystical and holy—in Christianity there is the Holy Trinity, Jesus rising from the dead on the third day, three wise men with three gifts; and then there are the three holy cities in Islam, the three Patriarchs in Judaism, the Three Pure Ones in Taoism, etc.—but there's really nothing I can find in *The Encyclopedia of Religion* about the significance of multiplying threes in order to attain a "holy" number.

"I learned, for example, that the ninth order of heaven is where God himself resides." Factual Dispute: Are we talking about Dante here? Because according to Dante, God resides not *in* but *beyond* the ninth sphere of heaven, in what's called the Empyrean (*Divine Comedy* by Dante Alighieri, Canto XXX, by way of *Bartleby.com*).

"That before he could receive the secret meaning of runes, Odin had to hang for nine days on a tree." Factual Quibble: Odin actually hanged for "Nine Days and Nights," not just nine days (source: "Odin's Nine Nights" by Jennifer Emick, *About.com*).

"That there are always nine Muses alive at any time." Confirmed: Calliope, Clio, Erato, Euterpe, Melpomene, Polyhymnia, Terpsichore, Thalia, and Urania (source: *Godchecker.com*).

"Always nine Maidens in ancient Celtic myths." Confirmed by the *Encyclopedia Mythica*.

"Always nine floors in the most sacred Buddhist temples." Almost confirmed: It's not so much the "most sacred Buddhist temples" that have nine stories as it is the single "most sacred Buddhist temple." From *BuddhaNet.net*: "Before his death, the Buddha enjoined his followers to make pilgrimages to four sites: Lumbini, where he was born; Uruvela (modern Bodh Gaya), the site of his enlightenment; Sarnath, the place of his first sermon; and Kushinara, where he died. Each of these sites may be visited today, and Bodh Gaya remains the most sacred of the four . . . It consists of a high straight-edged pyramidal tower of nine stories."

"If a servant finds nine peas in a pod and places that pod on the floor of her kitchen, the first man who comes in and tramples that pod will be the man she marries." Confirmed: I was able to find a random website that says: "If a girl found nine peas in a pod, she would place it at the door, and the next available man to come through the door would be her future husband." Close enough.

"Nine knots in a string of wool will cure a broken ankle." Factual Dispute: According to an article entitled "Cape Breton/Uist Folklore: I Have a Charm for You" by Allan Gillis, there are two significant references to the magical powers of knots in wool, but neither of them matches up with what John is saying. First, Gillis cites an anecdote from Pliny who reported that "some people cured diseases of the groin by taking a thread from a spider's web, tying nine knots on it, and then fastening it to the patient's groin; but to make the cure effectual it was necessary to name some widow as each knot was tied." And then that "sprains were cured by an old woman saying a rhyme over the injured member, or by placing around the sprain a string made from white spool thread knotted with seven knots." So: close. But no folkloric cigar.

"Nine grains of wheat on a four-leaf clover will lure a Victorian faerie." Factual Dispute: Almost everywhere I've looked—which predictably includes a lot of poorly constructed websites about faeries—suggests that seven grains of wheat are what will catch a faerie, not nine.

"Possession, after all, is nine-tenths of the law." We do say this. But it's also more formally confirmed in "Nine-Tenths of the Law: English Copyright Debates and the Rhetoric of the Public Domain" by Mark Rose in *Law and Contemporary Problems* 66, no. 75 (2003): 75–87.

"To look nine ways is to squint." Confirmed: *Dictionary of Phrase and Fable* by E. Cobham Brewer, 1898.

"To be right as ninepence is to be doing very well." Confirmed: *World Wide Words*, 1996.

"To be dressed to the nines is to be looking great." Confirmed: *World Wide Words*.

Nine grains of wheat on a four-leaf clover will lure a Victorian faerie.

Possession, after all, is nine-tenths of the law.

To look nine ways is to squint.

To be right as ninepence is to be doing very well.

To be dressed to the nines is to be looking great.

And to be on cloud nine is to be feeling high, a phrase that originated, folklorists say, when the United States Weather Bureau divided all clouds into nine different levels, the highest of which, at 30,000 feet, are called cumulonimbus. These are the fluffy ones, the mountainous ones, the ones usually seen on sunny summer days, and which also are the cause of storms.

"And to be on cloud nine is to be feeling high, a phrase that originated, folklorists say, when the United States Weather Bureau divided all clouds into nine different levels, the highest of which, at 30,000 feet, are called cumulonimbus. These are the fluffy ones, the mountainous ones, the ones usually seen on sunny summer days, and which also are the cause of storms." Kind of Confirmed: While folklorists at *World Wide Words* confirm that this is the meaning of the phrase "on cloud nine," there is nothing else in John's story that adds up. First of all, there are more than nine classes of clouds. According to the University of Denver's Department of Meteorology, there are ten types, including "cirrus, cirrostratus, cirrocumulus, altocumulus, altostratus, stratocumulus, stratus, nimbostratus, cumulus, and cumulonimbus." Second of all, the University of Illinois at Champaign–Urbana claims on its Department of Atmospheric Studies website that cumulonimbus clouds can actually reach up to 40,000 feet, not 30,000, and Plymouth State University's Meteorology Program says that they've even been recorded as high as 60,000 feet. Meanwhile, NASA says that cumulonimbus clouds aren't even the highest. There's apparently a rare form of cloud called "the noctilucent cloud" that can be found at 278,800 feet. So, maybe John wants to rephrase this to say "the United States Weather Bureau divided all clouds into a number of different levels, among the highest of which are called cumulonimbus"?

I think we knew, however, that he really fell for eight.

Drove back to where they lived.

Made plans for dinner soon.

Kissed and hugged and waved goodbye and said we'd be in touch.

I left Las Vegas five months after Levi Presley died.

At some point it came clear while I was visiting the Presleys that in fact I had not spoken to their son the night he died.

It was clear as I left Vegas that some other boy had called.

Clear that if I point to something seeming like significance there is the possibility that nothing real is there.

Sometimes we misplace knowledge in pursuit of information.

Sometimes our wisdom, too, in pursuit of what's called knowledge.

"Levi came home at 2:00 a.m. . . . 'But then again we had just grounded him.'" The Coroner's Report goes along with this basic chronology: "Clark County Medical Examiner Hank Missig made notification to decedent's parents at their residence. They [Gayle and Levi Presley] informed him the decedent had come home early this morning and was suspected of smoking

L evi came home at 2:00 a.m., or he came home at 2:30 a.m. But neither Gail, his mom, nor Levi Senior, his dad, can remember exactly which. This doesn't matter, though, they both say, because his curfew was 11:00. "We didn't say anything immediately because he had a tournament the next day, and we knew he needed his sleep," Gail says. Levi slept for five hours or he slept for four and a half hours, then he woke, showered, dressed, ate nothing, drove to his tournament,

marijuana. The decedent had a karate tournament to attend this afternoon and he did not do well. At about 1700 hours, after the decedent went home after the tournament, his father advised him that he was grounded because of his activity earlier in the morning. The decedent then ran out of the house, got into his vehicle and drove away."

"Levi drove east down Pleasant Plains Way, turned right onto Rainy River, left onto Joe Michael, right onto Shermcreft, right onto Gowan, left onto Rainbow, right onto Cheyenne, south onto Interstate 15 past two exits, then left onto Sahara, left onto Vegas, left onto Baltimore, and right into the parking garage at the Stratosphere Hotel." He

stretched, cheered, competed, lost, drove back home, slammed the car door, slammed the front door, slammed his room door, and stayed there. "He was probably in there two hours," Gail says. Is that unusual? "That's not unusual," she says, "but after a tournament I guess it'd be a little unusual, because he really liked to talk about his meets when he came home." After another hour Gail says she and her husband called Levi into their bedroom and told him that he was grounded for staying out past his curfew and for being at a party to which, they suspected, other kids had brought drugs. Gail says she heard Ecstasy. Levi Senior says pot. Levi said fine, threw his cell phone on their bed and told them that they might as well take that too. He slammed their bedroom door, slammed the front door, slammed his car door, and drove away. Is that unusual? "That's not unusual, he's a teenager," says Gail. "But then again we had just grounded him." Levi drove east down Pleasant

would have needed to take a left on Cheyenne, not a right, and then go 7.5 miles south on I-95 before reaching the 15. Otherwise, if Levi had turned right onto Cheyenne he would never have hit the 15, and thus never made it to the Stratosphere. Also, in order to reach Sahara from I-15 South, one needs to take a left on Sahara, because the casino is east of the freeway.

Plains Way, turned right onto Rainy River, left onto Joe Michael, right onto Shermcreft, right onto Gowan, left onto Rainbow, right onto Cheyenne, south onto Interstate 15 past two exits, then left onto Sahara, left onto Vegas, left onto Baltimore, and right into the parking garage at the Stratosphere Hotel. He found a space on the fifth level, the blue level, three spaces away from the elevator. It was 5:18 p.m. Levi then either walked down two flights of stairs to the third level of the garage, the orange level of the garage, where a skywalk connects parking to the hotel's registration. Or, he may have waited there to take the elevator. This was Saturday, however, and in the early evening hours on Saturdays in Vegas the elevators everywhere are slow. Once inside the casino, Levi walked down its red carpeted staircase and passed the Group Tours reception desk on his right

"He found a space on the fifth level, the blue level, three spaces away from the elevator." No evidence of this in John's notes. **I can confirm that there are non-handicapped parking spots three spaces away from the elevator, however, and that the fifth level is indeed the blue level, so this is at least potentially correct.** However, when I was there on a Saturday morning in the early autumn, almost the entire fifth level was already full. I can only imagine how much more busy it would be on a Saturday evening during the summer. It seems a stroke of fate that he'd be able to get that space. John, where is this information coming from?

John: Your nitpicking is absurd and it's ruining this essay. So, as I've said, I'm not participating. Good luck.

Jim: In other words, you're taking your ball and going home. Very mature. You know, confirming factual details so that a piece like this has some semblance of accuracy isn't "nitpicking," and I think most readers would agree with me. This process is actually meant to help enhance your writing. But I can't imagine you could appreciate anything that would require you to alter your precious words, which no doubt fell into the world from your pen fully formed and immaculate.

John: Yeah, I'm the immature one.

"It was 5:18 p.m." According to the Coroner's Report, Levi jumped from the tower at 6:01 p.m. The report also says that he left his house at about 5:00 p.m. Google Maps estimates that the trip from his house to the Stratosphere is 12.6 miles, or about 17 minutes, and it's a fair guess that he was probably speeding. So on its surface, John's claim for "5:18 p.m." is somewhat reasonable. However, as noted earlier, Vegas puts L.A. to shame in terms of traffic. So in order for this time line to be feasible, Levi either left his house earlier than the Coroner's Report states, or he hit nothing but green lights all the way, and lucked into a peculiarly light patch of traffic on the highway.

"Levi then either walked down two flights of stairs to the third level of the garage, the orange level of the garage, where a skywalk connects parking to the hotel's registration. Or, he may have waited there to take the elevator. This was Saturday, however, and in the early evening hours on Saturdays in Vegas the elevators everywhere are slow." I can confirm that this is the path one must take from the fifth level of the parking garage into the casino, as well as the orangeness of level three, the existence of the skywalk, and the noticeably slow elevators on Saturday nights. However, Levi was a sixteen-year-old guy, and the flights of stairs between these parking levels are quite short. I think it's unlikely that an impatient kid would wait to take a crowded elevator if he was in the frame of mind that he probably was in.

"Once inside the casino, Levi walked down its red carpeted staircase . . ." When I made the walk, the staircase was faded purple, not red.

". . . and passed the Group Tours reception desk on his right side . . ." Confirmed: on the right.

"... and Roxy's Diner on his left . . ." But Roxy's Diner isn't directly across from the Group Tours desk. It's a misstatement to suggest that if Levi turned right he would have seen the Group Tours desk and then if he'd turned left he would have seen Roxy's. They are a good distance apart from one another.

"... where a disk jockey plays fifties rock and the waitstaff sings." They do in fact sing, like nightingales.

"Because it was a Saturday and early evening at Roxy's 'the place definitely would have been hopping,' said their featured waiter, Johnny Pot

side and Roxy's Diner on his left, where a disk jockey plays fifties rock and the waitstaff sings. Because it was a Saturday and early evening at Roxy's "the place definitely would have been hopping," said their featured waiter, Johnny Pot Roast, who thinks he was on duty that night, he said. "And who knows, I was probably singing 'Greased Lightning,' 'cause it's a high-energy number and that's what we want on a Saturday night." When Johnny starts singing the waitresses pull microphones from the pouches of their aprons and jump onto the partitions between the diner's booths. They wave their order pads in the air and shimmy in place while diners lift forkfuls of potatoes to their

Roast, who thinks he was on duty that night, he said. 'And who knows, I was probably singing "Greased Lightning," 'cause it's a high-energy number and that's what we want on a Saturday night.'" A brief interview with Johnny Pot Roast appears in John's notes, and this is a rough paraphrase of what he said. So it's acceptable.

"... while diners lift forkfuls of potatoes to their mouths . . ." Factual Dispute: It's more of a burgers-and-fries kind of place, rather than a pot-roast-and-potatoes kind of place, so this would be an inaccurate description of the restaurant's fare.

"Levi then walked past the casino's forty-eight card tables and 1,200 slot machines . . ." The Stratosphere's website claims that the hotel "boasts an 80,000-square-foot casino featuring over fifty table games and more than 1,500 of the hottest slot and video poker machines." And a press release from 2001 says that there are "1,600 slot machines along with a plethora of table games . . ." As of October 2006, when I visited, there were five roulette tables, four craps tables, and forty card tables on the main floor. So, in this case, neither John's estimate nor the hotel's own claim is correct, unless there are some tables hidden in a high-stakes back room or something. But we're talking about the Stratosphere here . . .

". . . some of which are named after popular American television shows—I DREAM OF JEANNIE, WHEEL OF FORTUNE, HOGAN'S HEROES—and some of which are named after popular American merchandise—SPAM, HARLEY-DAVIDSON, the board game BATTLESHIP—and some of which are not named after anything at all— PRESS YOUR LUCK, THE NICKEL GAME, PUSH IT PUSH IT PUSH IT . . ." I never saw any of these during my visit, but I'm going to give a pass to this issue of slot machines because I think this is a case in which the effort to track down the right information far outweighs the need for factual confirmation of something that I'm 99 percent sure John won't bother changing anyway. It should be noted however that *Press Your Luck* was a television game show that ran from 1983 to 1986, and so a slot machine named after it is hardly "not named after anything." The show has actually become something of a cult classic. I watched it a lot as a child and have pretty vivid memories of it. So maybe this should be altered to acknowledge the slot machine's connection to the TV show and that it therefore is not "not anything at all." But again, I doubt John's going to be changing much of anything at this point. John, have you ever watched TV, or would that ruin your artistic sensibility?

John: You've missed the point through this entire essay, Jim.

Jim: Hey, a response!

John: It really and truly does not matter that there

mouths and Johnny jumps high and lands on his knees and holds his eyes shut as he holds the long *ing* in the long final high note in "lightning." Levi then walked past the casino's forty-eight card tables and 1,200 slot machines, some of which are named after popular Ameri-

was a short-running television show that could or could not have been the source for the name of this slot machine. (And "press your luck" has existed as an idiom in our culture for a lot longer than the 1980s, by the way, so I wouldn't flatter that favorite TV show of yours with being the inspiration for this game.) Anyway, the point I would like to state for the record is that there are of course hundreds of details that could be accurately or inaccurately reported about the scenery Levi passed in the last few minutes of his life. But all of it is tremendously trifling when you consider what's about to happen.

Jim: I don't disagree that these facts are trifling, John, but don't you think that the gravity of the situation demands an accuracy that you're dismissing as incidental? This isn't just about the name of one slot machine. I mean, even if there was no inherent meaning in these details, you're giving them meaning by calling attention to them. You basically made this same point earlier when you pissed all over me about the history of Tae Kwon Do. You are writing what will probably become the de facto story of what happened to Levi, and so every detail you choose to do that with will become significant, because your account will be the one account anyone is ever likely to read about him. And that's why to me this is serious business, because the record you're creating now, however minor, will be regarded as the authoritative one, if only because there is no competing narrative anyone else is likely to read or write about this kid. You've said yourself that what you're making is art, and *ars longa, vita brevis,* no? Why not suck it up and do the work to get it right?

John: It's not that I'm claiming there's no meaning in this flood of information, Jim, but rather that the more important thing to highlight here is the *search* for meaning. And an integral part of my search for that meaning is this attempt to reconstruct details in a way that makes them feel significant, even if that significance is one that doesn't naturally occur in the event being described. And I know full well that by saying something like that I will make a lot of people uncomfortable, but this is what I believe the job of the artist is. I am seeking a truth here, but not necessarily accuracy. I think it's very misleading for us to continue pretending that nonfiction writers have a mystically different relationship with "The Truth" than any other kind of writer. Because we don't. What we do have, like every other artist, is a compulsion for meanings, and so, just as any other artist would, we arrange things and we alter details and we influence interpretations as we pursue ideas. I know that most hard-core nonfiction writers won't agree with this, and that's fine. I know that I'm in the minority. But I also suspect that those are the kinds of writers who still have faith in genre, who have faith in the idea that by calling themselves "nonfiction" writers they automatically are, or that by calling their texts "nonfiction" they automatically are. And bless their hearts for having that kind of faith, really, because somebody's got to keep up the struggle to try to nail down the facts of the world, to construct the sorts of histories you mentioned earlier. But that doesn't mean that I think that they're going to find those facts, just as I don't think that my mom is going to find the God that she's been looking for all her life. But neither does it mean that I think her effort is pointless. It's just not my effort. Those who embrace the idea of "non-fiction" are very welcome to it, and I wish them every joy in the world in that pursuit—genuinely. But please don't hold me to parameters for making essays that I've had no say in establishing, that I wholly disagree with, and that I believe misrepresent the true purpose of this genre. An essay is an attempt, Jim. Nothing else. And fundamentally, for centuries, that's all it's been. Even etymologically, "essay" means "an attempt." And so, as a writer of essays, my interpretation of that charge is that I try—that I *try*—to take control of something before it is lost entirely to chaos. That's what I want to be held accountable for as a writer; it's how I want to be judged. Others can request to be judged by how strenuously they have tried to get their facts right, but for me, personally, that's not exciting work. And neither does it seem like it would result in particularly consequential art.

Jim: I don't know . . . I hear you, I really do, but I'm just having a visceral reaction to this, and I know it's making me sound like I'm not hip to the last hundred years of artistic experimentation, but I'm still uneasy with the ramifications of what you're saying. I am with you in that I don't necessarily believe that a "nonfiction" essay has to strive for an objective account of an occurrence as its primary project, or that the

can television shows—I DREAM OF JEANNIE, WHEEL OF FORTUNE, HOGAN'S HEROES—and some of

writer is ethically obligated to secure the reality of an event in cultural memory. And I'm all for the PoMo-historiographic-metafictional appropriation of events and personages. But there still seems to be something strange about doing this sort of thing with someone like Levi, who was just a teenager, after all, just a kid in Las Vegas—not a cultural figure or an icon whose life is for the taking and can be radically manipulated and reinterpreted. I mean, clearly it's not like you're defiling his grave by propagating these inaccuracies, but it's kind of like you're being dishonest about where that grave is.

John: Why on earth would we care about where his grave is? I swear to god that's the least interesting thing this essay could concern itself with. And it's definitely not where this essay is trying to locate itself. This isn't a profile about a boy's suicide and the particular inner demons that brought that death about. This essay is about an idea, and Levi represents that idea. Now, is it crass to call a dead boy whom I never knew an "idea"? Probably. But would it be better to call him a "subject"? A "character"? He's going to be "used"—or "defiled," as you put it—the moment he's written about. So maybe the most ethically appropriate thing for me to have done is to have completely made up a suicide victim so that I could use him however I wished. But I have a feeling that we'd still be having this argument even if I'd done that. I understand your concerns, Jim—I completely do. I don't know for certain whether it's right for an essay to do this kind of work. But what I believe is that unless the imagination can do this, then I don't know what it's for. What writing isn't fueled by the imagination? Would we even want to read a work of literature that wasn't engaged with the imagination?

Jim: Great, so now if I have reservations about what you're doing, then I'm against imaginative writing? That's obviously not what I'm saying, John. I'm not saying that you need to have—or even pretend to have—some hallowed relationship to "The Truth" in your writing, but it does seem like there's a line that you should be wary of crossing in a work that you're calling "nonfiction." And no, I don't think that it's crass to call Levi an idea or a subject or a character, because all of those things describe how he's being used in this essay. I'm just saying that there is something that feels strange about labeling your narrative "nonfiction" while you're willfully manipulating facts. While I may know that when you claim that something you've written is "nonfiction" you don't necessarily mean that it's "not fictional," can you at least see why others might feel otherwise if they don't know what they're getting into? I suspect that when you label a factually inaccurate text "nonfiction" you do so with the intention of calling into question the whole idea of that term. But when people who haven't read your manifestos on the subject pick up something like this and see it labeled as nonfiction, can you see how they might take it to be an indicator of a totally different sort of intentionality? By doing that you initiate a social contract that says you understand that by calling your work nonfiction—even the kind that embellishes certain "soft" details or makes use of the imagination to describe how things "feel" or what things "seem" like—you will stop short of saying things that you know are blatantly untrue.

John: All right, number one: I'm not calling this "nonfiction," and neither do I tend to call anything that I write "nonfiction," because I don't accept that term as a useful description of anything that I value in literature. The only reason this is being labeled "nonfiction" by your editors is because that is one of the two binary categories that editors allow in prose. And second, Jim, please keep in mind that we are talking about the name of a slot machine here.

Jim: We aren't talking about a slot machine, John, and you know it. Your essay delves into people's lives and livelihoods, bringing into question the moral status of an entire community of people, and it unleashes a parade of easily verifiable and yet clearly manipulated facts in order to make its point.

John: The fact that you think that there's so clear a connection between "the moral status of a community" and "easily verifiable facts" is the problem with this exercise. Numbers and stats can only go so far in illustrating who a person is or what a community is about. At some point, we must as writers leap into the skin of a person or a community in an attempt to embody them. That's obviously an incredibly violent procedure, but I think that unless we're willing to do that as writers (and go along for that ride as readers), then we're not actually doing our job.

Jim: I'm not saying that I think writing has to be science, or that there are rules for what "can" and "cannot" be done, or a formula for how to do it. I am, however, saying that there is "The Truth" and then there are localized "truths," and then there are "soft facts," and

then there are "hard facts," and I'm not sure why you seem intent on pretending that they're all the same thing, that they're all equally arbitrary, because they're not. The point I'm trying to make is less an artistic point and more of a socio-political and psychological point. It seems to me like it's important for a person to know whether what they're reading is the product of someone trying to "keep up the struggle to nail down the facts of the world," as you put it, or if they're reading something that disregards, discards, or manipulates those facts for artistic purposes. People feel like they've been trifled with if they discover they've been misled on that front. I mean, the whole point of all these shit storms over the last ten years that keep popping up every time someone finds out that a memoir was "embellished" isn't that the reading public doesn't understand that writers sometimes "use their imaginations." It's about people searching for some sort of Truth that connects with how they feel about themselves and their place in the world, finding that Truth in a piece of writing that resonates with them deeply, and then being devastated when they find out that the thing they were inspired by turned out to be deliberately falsified, as in not just reinterpreted and poetically embellished, but explicitly falsified for seemingly self-aggrandizing purposes. And so they end up feeling alone in the world all over again.

John: Is that what I'm doing in this essay, Jim? Am I "embellishing" for "self-aggrandizing purposes"?

Jim: I'm not saying that that's what you're doing in this essay, but the anarchic approach to "truth" that you seem to be advocating is certainly not helping anything.

John: But since when did a little intellectual anarchy become a bad thing? Since when did we start allowing rules to dictate what is valid in art? Don't we purposely afford the artist with liberties that aren't usually allowed in everyday discourse? I mean, isn't that one of the reasons we turn to art? Don't we expect the artist to test limits, to challenge the rules, to break taboos? Art is invested with special privileges in our culture because we believe it serves a special role. It's there to challenge us. Rules of any kind do not apply to art, they don't belong in art—even when art causes "shit storms." In fact, I'd say one of art's jobs is to incite shit storms.

Jim: The inner punk in me agrees: Artistically and philosophically, when we're talking about that status of "truth" in language and art on a basic level I think

which are named after popular American merchandise—SPAM, HARLEY-DAVIDSON, the board game

more or less that I agree with what you're saying. As two terminally overeducated dudes, I'm sure that you and I both are confident in our knowledge that Nietzsche calls truth a "mobile army of metaphors, metonymies, anthropomorphisms," that both God and the Author are dead, that we all make our own truths and shape our own realities, that The Man is invested in keeping any non-institutional viewpoints down . . . But while it's all well and good for us to pat ourselves on the back for how subversive and avant-garde we are, when you step back and look at what you're really saying isn't there something very rarified and academic about that? I applaud anyone's search for The Truth, The Artistic Truth, or any other kind of Truth that you can finagle this argument to be about, but when you change the factual qualities of a thing to suit your own artistic interests, you're creating something that never existed—not the truth about Las Vegas or the truth about Levi Presley, but the truth about "John D'Agata's Las Vegas" and "John D'Agata's Levi Presley." Which is not an unworthy artistic endeavor, to be sure, but don't you see how there might be something fundamentally wrong with trying to pass off "John D'Agata's Las Vegas" as a factual report of "The 'Real' Las Vegas," without giving readers at least a wink or a nod?

BATTLESHIP—and some of which are not named after anything at all—

John: I've been giving readers winks and nods for my entire career, Jim. I've edited anthologies, I've written essays, I've given lectures, I've taught courses . . . all about this issue. At some point the reader needs to stop demanding that they be spoon-fed like infants and start figuring out on their own how to deal with art that they disagree with—and how to do so without throwing a fucking temper tantrum or banning that art from ever appearing again.

Jim: Great, another writer who despises his readers.

John: I don't despise readers, Jim, but why do we turn to art if we're going to demand to know up front "what we're getting into"? If we're going to ask literature to guarantee that we aren't going to be "trifled with" or "misled"? You're talking about shopping-mall art. You're talking about the kinds of art consumers who wrote to Oprah Winfrey after discovering that James Frey had made up some of his memoir's details, and then demanded that she publicly chastise him because they felt betrayed. It's these same people who made that book a best-seller, and it's these same people who seemed unable to recognize that the experience that that book had given them—an experience

for which they and Oprah and all of those dozens upon dozens of reviewers had once celebrated his book—was really the only responsibility Frey had to them: *to give them a good experience.* Now, some of us might not be able to understand how on earth that book could have affected so many people because it wasn't particularly good (not even with his embellishments) but that doesn't matter. People liked it. People found something in it that felt transcendent for them. And that's what art is supposed to do.

Jim: But clearly those people were looking for more than just a "good experience," otherwise why would they have gotten so upset about learning the reality behind its artifice? That's the whole point I was trying to make before . . .

John: Because we're adolescent when it comes to art. We've almost entirely disenfranchised art in our public schools, in our homes, in our culture at large. Of course we're going to stomp our feet and scream when we're suddenly thrown a curveball after emotionally opening ourselves up to something and then learning that that thing isn't exactly what it seems. And of course that's going to feel like a betrayal, because we don't have enough deep experiences with art to know that that is what art is for: to break us open, to make us raw, to destabilize our understanding of ourselves and of our world so that we can experience both anew, with fresh eyes, and with therefore the possibility of recognizing something that we had not recognized before. Art is supposed to change us, to challenge us, and yes, even to trick us. What Frey's audience was responding to so vehemently was the sensation of having had a genuine experience with art. And they freaked out. And they tarred and feathered a guy for having given them an experience they felt unprepared for. But whose fault was that?

Jim: It's his readers' fault? You're calling his readers ignorant?

John: I am calling his readers ignorant on a multitude of levels.

Jim: All right, let's go at this from a different angle. When someone watches the news or reads the paper or listens to the radio in search of "facts" about the world, is it strange that they should get upset when they're given news-as-entertainment, or when they're presented with something that is altered or made up for nefarious political or economic reasons?

John: No, that's a legitimate reason to be annoyed.

Jim: And don't you feel betrayed when people in

power say things that are out-and-out not true in order to serve their own purposes?

John: Sure.

Jim: So now, even though it's clear that there aren't any 100 percent reliable sources, can you agree with me that people should at least be able to hope for reliable intentions?

John: Yeah. But I'm not a politician, Jim. Nor am I reporter. And I'm also not the reader's boyfriend or daddy or therapist or priest or yoga instructor, nor anyone from whom they should be seeking a trustworthy relationship. Just because there are some parts of our culture in which we need to demand honesty and expect reliable intentions doesn't mean that it's appropriate for us to expect that from every experience we have in the world.

Jim: But even if nonfiction from the very beginning of its inception was based on "the strength of its argument rather than the precision of its evidence"—believe it or not, I've read your essays on the topic—that doesn't change the fact that people are going to get upset when someone wins them over with a powerful argument, and then reveals that they employed fraudulent evidence to do so.

John: What we're dancing around here is the idea of a moral responsibility in nonfiction. And that's why this sort of conversation always gets me peeved—and why the conversation also always ends up in circles—because the moment we start judging a form of art in terms of its "moral value" is the moment we stop talking about art. Just by having this conversation and raising these issues we are disenfranchising nonfiction as literarature. And this is frustrating, because we would never be having this conversation about a work of poetry or fiction or drama. Those are literary genres that we recognize, without any question, as *literary*. As artful. But nonfiction has been struggling to distinguish itself as art for decades in our culture.

Jim: Well, those are literary genres that don't make explicit claims of factual accuracy. Right or wrong, John, people are going to have different expectations of something that's called "nonfiction." There's a perceived difference in the intentionality behind nonfiction and fiction, because nonfiction is supposed to have its feet firmly planted in reality. Isn't that the definition of "nonfiction"?

John: Why do you have such a hard-on for that term? I'm not using that term to describe this essay, you are.

Jim: Because like or not, it's what the world calls the genre that you're working in. Maybe it's the fault of the language—we don't have enough words for snow or the variety of literary experiences—but your definition of an "essay" is an idiosyncratic one that is not shared with the public at large. I'm not saying that that's a good thing or a bad thing, but it's a thing.

John: Well, then there's another reason why we need a better-educated culture. The fact is that "nonfiction" was first widely used in literary circles only fifty or sixty years ago. It was introduced to describe the work that was being done in "New Journalism" in the 1960s and 1970s. So our use of it is very new. And forget about the fact that not everything that was being written at that time in this genre was journalism. Obviously, there was memoir, there was biography, there was nature writing, travelogues, etc. So not only is "nonfiction" a very young term, but it's been an inadequate one from the start. And yet we've had the term "essay" at our disposal for over five hundred years. And appropriately enough, what the term "essay" describes is not a negation of genre—as "nonfiction" does—but rather an activity, "an attempt, a trial, an experiment." And so all of a sudden under that term you can feel the genre opening back up in order to embrace its own curiosity, trying to track the

PRESS YOUR LUCK, THE NICKEL GAME, PUSH IT PUSH IT PUSH IT—

activity of a practitioner's mind as it negotiates memories, observations, anecdotes, history, science, myth, experience . . . An essay is not a vehicle for facts, in other words, nor for information, nor verifiable experience. An essay *is* an experience, and a very human one at that. It's an enactment of the experience of trying to find meaning—an emotional meaning, an intellectual meaning, a political meaning, a scientific one, or whatever goal that artist has set for the text. And indeed, if we dig down into the history of essays we will find writers like Natalia Ginzburg and Mary McCarthy and George Orwell and Henry Thoreau and Charles Lamb and Thomas De Quincey and Daniel Defoe and Christine de Pisan and Sei Shōnagon and St. Augustine and Plutarch and Seneca and Cicero and Herodotus and dozens of other masters of this form who regularly altered facts in order to get a closer understanding of what they were experiencing. Now, is that morally acceptable? Well, in some of their cultures it actually does seem to have been acceptable. But in the case of other writers, their manipulations of facts have gone entirely unnoticed. So does this mean we should now say that the essays that these writers have left us—some of which form the very foundation of this genre—are less worthy of our appreciation? I would hope not. Because the authenticity of Herodotus's musings about the world shouldn't have any bearing on how those musings make us feel. He's trying to instill wonder in us, not our approval for the accuracy of his facts. I guess my point is that if we were to return to a description of this genre that defined it according to its most inherent activity—one of curious investigation, rather than the fulfillment of some arbitrary sense of veracity—then I think we would be less inclined to make moral judgments about the choices writers make in this genre, and start instead appreciating those choices as efforts on behalf of literature.

Jim: This is getting nowhere; we seem to be talking past each other. I'm not saying that those kinds of essays are not worthy as art. And neither am I saying that they are poor examples of literature because they are not strictly factual. And I was never saying that they are morally reprobate because of that. What I'm saying is that, looking at them from the point of view of a fact-checker, and strictly in terms of what's verifiable in them, they are not great examples of things that are "not fictional."

John: Fine. And thank you, because I doubt that they would want to be considered "great examples of things that are not fictional." I don't want my stuff judged that way either.

Jim: But I am also saying that if they were presented to me as "not fictional" texts, I would feel misled by them.

John: Fair enough.

Jim: Fair enough?

John: You would feel misled. Sure.

Jim: So that's it?

John: Jim, you feel misled by my essay. I accept that. You feel that it's inappropriate for me to have done this. While I feel that it's a necessary part of my job to do this; that what I'm doing by taking these liberties is in fact making a better work of art—and thus a better and truer experience for the reader—than I could have if I'd stuck to the facts. So, fine. We disagree. I'm OK with that. But I'm also not sure where else to go.

and then Levi walked toward the woman at the foot of the escalator who sells cigarettes and cigars and battery-operated necklaces from a small tray that hangs from her shoulders below her breasts. There is a blue star necklace and a red orb necklace and a yellow cross necklace available for sale, each of which glows steadily or flickers randomly or even can be programmed "to reflect your own mood!" Amy, who was

". . . then Levi walked toward the woman at the foot of the escalator who sells cigarettes and cigars and battery-operated necklaces from a small tray that hangs from her shoulders below her breasts. There is a blue star necklace and a red orb necklace and a yellow cross necklace available for sale, each of which glows steadily or flickers randomly or even can be programmed 'to reflect your own mood!'" This is in John's notes. Although technically what he wrote is that there was a "Red Cross Necklace" and a "Yellow Orb Necklace," so he appears to have altered things a bit. I'm also pretty skeptical that a toy necklace could be programmed as sophisticatedly as John's describing. I also couldn't find any women selling such things when I was there.

"Then he went up the escalator. Levi would have stood in line at the hotel's ticket booth in order to buy a ticket to the top of the hotel's tower. Because it was Saturday and early evening, however, there would have been a long line at the hotel ticket booth. Levi would have stood between the fanny packs and the midriffs and the open containers and the flip-flops . . ." Even when I was there at around 11:00 a.m. on a Saturday I saw plenty of flip-flops, midriffs, and yes even open containers. So this is confirmed. People in Vegas don't waste any time.

". . . and noticed the backlit advertisements behind the hotel's ticket booth . . ." As previously noted, there are multiple entrances to the Stratosphere. There is the "Main Escalator" (Escalator #1) and the secondary "Escalator to the Top of the World Restaurant & Lounge & Tower of Shops Mall" (Escalator #2). If you use the entrance John is claiming Levi took (Escalator #2), there are no advertisements behind the ticket booth that it leads to, although there are some backlit ads on the wall adjacent to the ticket booth. The area with the most pronounced backlit advertisements is behind the ticket booth near the top of Escalator #1, which isn't the one John says Levi took. But, if Levi had taken Escalator #1, he wouldn't have walked past all of the

on duty that night, knows Levi didn't buy anything because she would have remembered a boy buying a necklace, she said. "Usually the guys who buy stuff are buying stuff for raves, and I always ask them where they're going 'cause I'm a raver, too." Then he went up the escalator. Levi would have stood in line at the hotel's ticket booth in order to buy a ticket to the top of the hotel's tower. Because it was Saturday and early evening, however, there would have been a long line at the hotel ticket booth. Levi would have stood between the fanny packs and the midriffs and the open containers and the flip-flops and noticed the backlit advertisements behind the hotel's ticket booth for the upcoming Billy Ray Cyrus concert in September or the Heavyweight Boxing

card tables; then again, if he went up Escalator #2, he wouldn't have walked past all of the stores in the Tower of Shops Mall, which John describes later on. So it's starting to appear that the path John's describing isn't actually possible, unless Levi came out of the parking garage, walked over to Escalator #2 (and thus past all of the card tables), and then looped back and took Escalator #1, going to the ticket booth with the advertisements and then past all the shops in the Tower of Shops Mall. That seems improbable, though. John probably combined these two routes into one so that he could get Levi to pass all this stuff and thus give us this catalogue of scenery.

". . . for the upcoming Billy Ray Cyrus concert in September . . ." There was a Billy Ray Cyrus concert on September 6 of that year, as confirmed by the Stratosphere's schedule of events.

". . . or the Heavyweight Boxing Extravaganza in November . . ." A Las Vegas boxing website suggests that an event that sounds like the one John is mentioning happened in September of that year, not November. And it was called a "Heavyweight Extravaganza," not a "Heavyweight Boxing Extravaganza," because I think "Boxing" was implied by the two large greased-up men wearing boxing gloves and grimacing at each other on the poster.

"... or the Stratosphere's New Guaranteed Refund Slot Program, which pays players back 15 percent of what they've lost ..." Confirmed in "Las Vegas Slot Club Refund Program" by Steve Bourie, *Gambling Times,* October–November 2002. But the program is severely limited in scope: "The program only applies to new 'slot club' members, is only valid for visitors to Las Vegas (residents of Las Vegas, North Las Vegas, Henderson, and Boulder City are not eligible), and you can only use [the refund] one time. To be eligible you need to sign up for a new Stratosphere Player's Club membership and then use your slot club card every time you play any slot or video poker machine. The casino will then reimburse fifteen percent of your coin-in (the total sum of money that is put in to play the machines), for any denomination from nickels up to $100, during the first thirty minutes of your play." So, maybe change "which pays players back fifteen percent of what they've lost" to "which in certain circumstances pays players back fifteen percent of what they've lost."

"... and then he would have purchased his ticket from one of the three ticket booth attendants for four dollars rather than six, because he was a Las Vegas resident ..." Factual Dispute: A hotel press release from that year claims "tower admission is $6 for adults and $4 for Nevada residents," so it would be inaccurate to say that the discount is available only to Las Vegas residents. Anyone in the state can get it.

"... and finally he would have begun to walk toward the tower's elevator at the other end of the Stratosphere's Tower of Shops Mall. Past Flagmania. Past Alpaca Pete's ... [etc.]" To begin with, the order of some of these shops is all wrong. And secondly, some

Extravaganza in November or the Stratosphere's New Guaranteed Refund Slot Program, which pays players back 15 percent of what they've lost, and then he would have purchased his ticket from one of the three ticket booth attendants for four dollars rather than six, because he was a Las Vegas resident, and finally he would have begun to walk toward the tower's elevator at the other end of the Stratosphere's Tower of Shops Mall. Past Flagmania. Past Alpaca Pete's. Past the Fabulous Las Vegas Magic Shop and the Great Wall of Magnets and Goldfather's, a kiosk that sells gold chains by the yard. Levi walked past Aqua Massage. Häagen-Dazs. Temporary Henna Airbrush Tattoo. Past Perfumania, Leather Land, Gifts Plus, Arcade. Past COMING SOON TO THIS LOCATION

of them don't even exist. Flagmania and Alpaca Pete's are confirmed.

"Past the Fabulous Las Vegas Magic Shop and the Great Wall of Magnets and Goldfather's, a kiosk that sells gold chains by the yard. Levi walked past Aqua Massage. Häagen-Dazs." The mall directory lists only "The Las Vegas Magic Shop," although the actual sign above the store calls it "The Fabulous Las Vegas Magic Shop." The discrepancy is acceptable then. I found no evidence whatsoever of a "Great Wall of Magnets," however. The Goldfather's kiosk sells "gold chains by the inch"—although technically speaking, I suppose if you sell something by the inch you are also, by extension, selling it by the yard. Häagen-Dazs is confirmed.

"Temporary Henna Airbrush Tattoo." As far as I can tell, henna can't really be applied by airbrush, although people who do temporary henna tattoos also tend to do temporary airbrush tattoos. So maybe this is OK. Who knows at this point?

"Past Perfumania . . ." Confirmed.

"... Leather Land ..." The mall directory refers to the store as Leatherland. Although here again the sign that's above the store reads "Leather Land."

"... Gifts Plus ..." Roger that.

"... Arcade ..." Check.

"Past COMING SOON TO THIS LOCATION ANOTHER EXCITING SHOP." I assume that by the time I visited the mall this exciting shop had already opened.

Past the Stitch It On's hat embroidery kiosk." It's not a kiosk, it's a full store.

"Past Vegas Candle's HUGE BLOW-OUT SALE! Past Wetzel's Prezels, Cleo's Fine Jewelers, and CJ's Casino Emporium, which sells 'vintage 1991' slot machines for $4,995." The shop referred to as "Vegas Candle" is actually called "Vegas Lights." CJ's Casino Emporium wasn't anywhere in sight when I visited. Plus, John's notes indicate that the slot machine he saw on sale was priced at $4,895, not $4,995. Wetzel's Prezels and Cleo's Fine Jewelers are confirmed.

"Levi walked past Breathe, an oxygen bar, where you can 'revive your body, renew your spirit, relax your mind, and feel more alive' for fifteen dollars per fifteen-minute dose . . ." According to John's notes, a fifteen-minute dose of oxygen at Breathe costs sixteen dollars, not fifteen.

ANOTHER EXCITING SHOP. Past the Stitch It On's hat embroidery kiosk. Past Vegas Candle's HUGE BLOW-OUT SALE! Past Wetzel's Prezels, Cleo's Fine Jewelers, and CJ's Casino Emporium, which sells "vintage 1991" slot machines for $4,995. Levi walked past Breathe, an oxygen bar, where you can "revive your body, renew your spirit, relax your mind, and feel more alive" for fifteen dollars per fifteen-minute dose, which includes your choice of one of eighteen complimentary oxygen aromas, such as Nirvana, Watermelon, Clarity, Peach, Sublime, Cappuccino, Synergy, Dream, Chocolate, Eclipse, Revitalize, or Tangerine. The girls at Breathe don't remember Levi stopping by the bar that

". . . which includes your choice of one of eighteen complimentary oxygen aromas, such as Nirvana, Watermelon, Clarity, Peach, Sublime, Cappuccino, Synergy, Dream, Chocolate, Eclipse, Revitalize, or Tangerine." John's notes list a lot more than eighteen aromas. Some of the others are Vanilla, Pumpkin Spice, Coconut, Strawberry, Clove, Lemon Grass, Pear, Watermelon, and Jasmine. I can't believe people pay green money for that crap.

"The girls at Breathe don't remember Levi stopping by the bar that evening, but they do recall hearing about his jump once it occurred. 'All I want to say,' said Jenny, who manages the bar, 'is that it's awful that it happened, but I know for a fact that he wasn't on O_2 when he did it.'" Jenny's name is not in John's notes. But her intimation that Levi was "not on O_2" is. That's such a ridiculous way to put it.

"Then Levi reached the end of the mall and walked down a ramp to wait in the next line. Because it was Saturday and early evening, however, there would have been a long line wrapping around the roped corrals four or five times and stretching back into the mall." Those corrals are metal, not "roped." Even with multiple entrances, though, there were people filling up seven wraparound lanes when I visited. It took me forty minutes to reach the elevator after I reached this point in the mall, even though the elevator was never more than fifty feet away from me. I suspect Levi would have waited in this line quite a bit longer than John is estimating, since he was there on a Saturday night.

"Harold, a security guard, eventually would have asked Levi if he had any metal in his pockets, and, because he did, Levi would have emptied his car keys into a white Stratosphere slot machine coin bucket, walked through the metal detector, picked up his keys, and walked into a narrow hallway to wait for the elevator to the tower." Confirmation of security guards at this post, as well as the metal detectors. The guard's name is not in John's notes, however.

evening, but they do recall hearing about his jump once it occurred. "All I want to say," said Jenny, who manages the bar, "is that it's awful that it happened, but I know for a fact that he wasn't on O_2 when he did it." Then Levi reached the end of the mall and walked down a ramp to wait in the next line. Because it was Saturday and early evening, however, there would have been a long line wrapping around the roped corrals four or five times and stretching back into the mall. Harold, a security guard, eventually would have asked Levi if he had any metal in his pockets, and, because he did, Levi would have emptied his car keys into a white Stratosphere slot machine coin bucket, walked through the metal detector, picked up his keys, and walked into a narrow hallway to wait for the elevator to the tower. Because it was Saturday and early evening, however, the group

"Because it was Saturday and early evening, however, the group with which Levi had waited in line would have had to wait in that hallway even longer. It would have been crowded and hot and yellow-lit that night, and for the long meanwhile during which Levi waited he might have glanced over the railing and seen below him the Stratosphere's amusement area that's called Strat-O-Fair, a passageway of carnival games beside the hotel's pool." The hall wasn't that crowded when I was there. I mean, there certainly wasn't a dearth of people around, but the real bottleneck is getting past the metal detectors; after that you're in a smaller line at the top of the passageway, where the elevator comes fairly regularly. I'm a bit confused, however, as to where this amusement area is supposed to be. I never saw anything like what John's describing. I don't think he's making it up, because I found a press release describing the attraction; I just couldn't find this area anywhere in the hotel.

"There is the softball-throwing game called 'Cat Splat' . . ." Confirmed in the press release.

". . . and the ring-throwing game called 'Orb-a-Toss' . . ." Supposed to be rendered "Orb-A-Toss," according to the press release.

". . . and the ride-at-your-own-risk mechanical bull that's called 'Vegas Cowboy': 'Warning! This mechanical bull is designed to simulate the motion of a live bull. Therefore, there is a high probability that the rider will be thrown from, and/or struck by, this mechanical bull. This mechanical bull is a heavy duty machine that will violently, erratically,

with which Levi had waited in line would have had to wait in that hallway even longer. It would have been crowded and hot and yellow-lit that night, and for the long meanwhile during which Levi waited he might have glanced over the railing and seen below him the Stratosphere's amusement area that's called Strat-O-Fair, a passageway of carnival games beside the hotel's pool. There is the softball-throwing game called "Cat Splat" and the ring-throwing game called "Orb-a-Toss" and the ride-at-your-own-risk mechanical bull that's called "Vegas Cowboy": "Warning! This mechanical bull is designed to simulate the motion of a live bull. Therefore, there is a high probability that the rider will be thrown from, and/or struck by, this mechanical bull. This mechanical bull is a heavy duty machine that will violently, erratically, and unpredictably spin and rotate the rider at high speeds. You must be at least thirteen years old to ride this

and unpredictably spin and rotate the rider at high speeds. You must be at least thirteen years old to ride this bull!'" Again, I couldn't find anything of the kind. But according to John's notes, the warning sign should actually read: "Warning! The mechanical bull is designed to simulate the motion of a live bucking bull. Therefore, there is a high probability that the rider will be thrown from, and/or struck by the mechanical bull. The mechanical bull is a heavy-duty machine, which will violently, erratically, and unpredictably spin and rotate the rider at high speeds. You must be at least fourteen years old to ride this bull! If you are pregnant you should not ride this bull."

"Then he entered the elevator. Inside, Levi would have been greeted by a young woman, perhaps Caroline, who would have worn black pants and a pink-and-teal Stratosphere polo shirt . . ." Nowadays the Stratosphere staff dress a little classier: black pants, white shirt, black windbreaker; or black pants, white shirt, and black vest; or tan polo shirt and black sport jacket. A description of the uniform during the nineties from *CheapoVegas.com* says, "Don't let anyone tell you that jewel tones are passé! At the Strat, everyone shimmers in the hues of rubies, amethysts and emeralds. Black vests with gold embroidery complement the change folks' red satin shirts, while the purple blouses worn by the dealers bring to mind some very flirty pirates. The cocktail waitresses are positively modest in their shiny violet mini-dresses . . ." Nothing really confirms the outfit John's describing, though.

". . . and who would have announced, once the doors had closed, that Levi and the elevator's other twenty-five-maximum occupants that night would soon be traveling 1,858-feet-per-minute to the top of the Stratosphere tower . . ." A Stratosphere press release claims that the speed of the elevator is 1,800-feet-per-minute, not 1,858, as John claims.

". . . even though they would only be traveling 857 feet to the top of the Stratosphere tower . . ." Confirmed on their website: the observation deck is on the 108th floor of the tower, which is 857 feet high. However, a press release from the hotel claims that the 108th floor is 854 feet high. So, something's screwed up in the hotel's own estimates.

bull!" Then he entered the elevator. Inside, Levi would have been greeted by a young woman, perhaps Caroline, who would have worn black pants and a pink-and-teal Stratosphere polo shirt, and who would have announced, once the doors had closed, that Levi and the elevator's other twenty-five-maximum occupants that night would soon be traveling 1,858-feet-per-minute to the top of the Stratosphere tower, even though they would only be traveling 857 feet to the top of the Stratosphere tower, together, in a double-decker elevator in which they would have been so closely arranged that it would have been impossible for them to have counted themselves, some of whom might have been drunk, some of whom might have been talking over the elevator operator's narrative of their ascent, and some of whom might have interrupted the operator to ask her, several times, on the same trip, while giggling, how many times each day she goes up and down the shaft. Then Levi would have exited and walked into the blue-lit hallway of the first level of the tower's two-level observation deck, past a closed gift

". . . together, in a double-decker elevator in which they would have been so closely arranged that it would have been impossible for them to have counted themselves, some of whom might have been drunk, some of whom might have been talking over the elevator operator's narrative of their ascent, and some of whom might have interrupted the operator to ask her, several times, on the same trip, while giggling, how many times each day she goes up and down the shaft." No proof of this in John's notes, but everyone loves a good dick joke, so I'll let it pass.

"Then Levi would have exited and walked into the blue-lit hallway of the first level of the tower's two-level observation deck . . ." It looks yellowish now, with the influence of a magenta light from around the elevator door spilling out into the space as well.

". . . past a closed gift shop, past a closed snack bar . . ." A lady folding shirts in the gift store up there said that they're usually open until 2:00 a.m., so surely it would have been open when Levi was up there at around 6:00 p.m. Ditto from the guy making pretzels in the snack bar. So maybe John's trying to create an eerie "ambience" of a deserted observation deck. I don't know. But it would be false to suggest that there isn't a lot of activity up there. The tower seems to be the Stratosphere's main attraction, so I suspect the hotel would want to keep as many stores open up there as possible.

". . . past the picture-paned radio station that had broadcast nothing for years . . ."** A guy I spoke with up there (who was wearing a suit and a name tag, so he had to have been official) didn't know what the room was for. Peeking into the windows, I saw a sign that said "Kool 93.1 2006 Summer of Fun Kickoff." There were CDs and microphones, but otherwise it just looked like a generic office. Kool 3.1's website says that it's located at "2880 Meade Ave, Suite #250, Las Vegas, Nevada 89102." So I don't know what's going on there.

". . . and into the carpeted round enclosure of the deck . . ." It is carpeted. And the top of the tower is very Space Needle-y, so I can confirm that the observation deck is indeed circular.

". . . floor-to-ceiling windows slant inward toward the ground so that visitors, while looking down at Las Vegas, toe-to-pane at the windows, might experience what pre-opening hotel press releases called, in 1994, 'free-fall.'" John's notes claim that this quote comes from a 1994 *Las Vegas Sun* article, not a press release from the hotel itself, so this is misattributed.

shop, past a closed snack bar, past the picture-paned radio station that had broadcast nothing for years, and into the carpeted round enclosure of the deck, whose floor-to-ceiling windows slant inward toward the ground so that visitors, while looking down at Las Vegas, toe-to-pane at the windows, might experience what pre-opening hotel press releases called, in 1994, "free-fall." Then he walked upstairs, outside. It was Saturday and early evening and there were many people around. Some kids running around the paved deck of the tower. Some adults looking through the coin-operated telescopes, making sure they wouldn't work before first depositing a coin. Some older people holding on to the inside chain-link fence of the deck, readjusting their grips each time a copter flew by. Levi walked left, east, away from where the sun had begun its own decline, and leaned briefly against the four-foot-high-railinged fence of the deck while a bride and groom took photographs of each other and then of the

"Then he walked upstairs, outside. It was Saturday and early evening and there were many people around. Some kids running around the paved deck of the tower. Some adults looking through the coin-operated telescopes, making sure they wouldn't work before first depositing a coin." Most of this is unconfirmable, as the activity on the deck would be determined by the individuals composing the crowd on the observation deck at any given time. I can confirm that there are coin-operated telescopes, however.

"Some older people holding on to the inside chain-link fence of the deck, readjusting their grips each time a copter flew by." The fence isn't chain-link; it's made of quarter-inch vertical bars.

"Levi walked left, east, away from where the sun had begun its own decline . . ." Confirmed: walking left out the door would take you in an easterly direction.

". . . and leaned briefly against the four-foot-high-railinged fence of the deck . . ." The Coroner's Report claims that the fence surrounding the inner perimeter of the deck is three feet and seven inches high, not "four feet" as John claims.

". . . while a bride and groom took photographs of each other and then of the view and then of the last three hundred feet of the tower above." A press release claims that the Outdoor Observation Deck at the Stratosphere is 869 feet high (one floor above the indoor part of the observation deck). However, the flyer they hand out to tourists at the top of the tower says that it's 866 feet high. Either way, though, the distance from the observation deck to the very top of the 1,149-foot tower is at most 283 and at least 280 feet, not 300 as John claims.

"Then Levi climbed over the four-foot-high-railinged fence, stepped into what Stratosphere security calls 'the moat,' a six-foot-wide concrete paved space between the four-foot-high fence on the deck's inside perimeter . . ." Correction: This moat, according to the Coroner's Report, is seven feet wide, as opposed to six, as John claims. Also, Levi wouldn't have been able to "step into" the moat, as there is a four-foot-ten-inch drop from the bottom of the fence onto this outer walkway. And the Coroner's Report explicitly states that there's an eight-foot-five-inch drop from the top of the short fence to the bottom of the walkway. So he would have had to "drop down" to it, not "step."

". . . and the ten-foot-high fence at the very edge of the perimeter, and then Levi climbed over the ten-foot-high fence and sat down." The outer fence is correctly reported as being ten feet.

"It was Saturday and early evening and an alarm was ringing in the hotel's security office." Confirmed that an alarm went off, according to the Coroner's Report.

"Levi sat on the ledge for forty-eight seconds before anyone on the deck walked by." Those forty-eight seconds are confirmed by the Coroner's Report. But there really isn't a ledge to sit on out there, so I'm not sure where Levi could have sat down. Beyond the outer fence there is sort of a halo-like metal ring attached to the base of the fence. Maybe that's what he sat on? But could it have held him?

"Now the sun was gone. Saturday was night. And the valley in which Levi had grown up became bright,

view and then of the last three hundred feet of the tower above. Then Levi climbed over the four-foot-high-railinged fence, stepped into what Stratosphere security calls "the moat," a six-foot-wide concrete paved space between the four-foot-high fence on the deck's inside perimeter and the ten-foot-high fence at the very edge of the perimeter, and then Levi climbed over the ten-foot-high fence and sat down. It was Saturday and early evening and an alarm was ringing in the hotel's security office. Levi sat on the ledge for forty-eight seconds before anyone on the deck walked by. Now the sun was gone. Saturday was night. And the valley in which Levi had grown up became bright, and it stayed bright, all the way

and it stayed bright, all the way to the invisible black mountains around it, the wall that would keep the city forever the shape it now was. Security officer Frank then approached Levi from the left, the east, and said 'Hey,' or he said 'Hey, kid,' or he said 'Kid, no,' or he said nothing, and it was his presence alone that caused Levi to turn his head to the left, stand up on the ledge, wave to the security officer, who does not appear on the screen of the video on which Levi is waving, and jump."** Levi allegedly also said "bye-bye" before jumping, according to the Coroner's Report.

But there are many more problems with this scenario as John's described it. First of all, the weather report says that it was "mostly cloudy" that night at 6:00 p.m., which complicates things, because if there were clouds obscuring the view that John is describing, then there's no way Levi could have looked out and seen anything in the distance. In addition, the sun set that night at approximately 7:58 p.m., Pacific Standard Time, which is two hours later than John says it had set, thus making his claim that "Now the sun was gone. Saturday was night" an impossibility, unless of course something was horrendously wrong with the rotation of the Earth that evening. Plus, looking out from the place from where Levi was likely to have jumped, it's clear that he would have been peering toward mountains that are brown, not black. However, there is a range of mountains whose name is "the Black Mountains," which John might be referring to, but if you follow the pathway John describes, these mountains would have been to Levi's right, not straight in front of him. The rest of the details about the security guard approaching Levi and what then transpired are confirmed by details that the Coroner's Report offers about the hotel's security video. But there are some things about this that make the accuracy of the Coroner's Report itself questionable, which causes some concern. For example, there are big questions that remain unanswered about the whole sequence of events leading up to Levi's death. The Coroner's Report states that "the decedent was witnessed by a hotel security officer jumping from the 109th floor observation deck of the Stratosphere Hotel & Casino," and that "the height from where the decedent jumped to where he landed was 833 feet." But, as noted earlier, level 8 of the observation deck, which is one floor beneath the level from which Levi jumped, is either 857 feet high or 854 feet high (depending on whether you believe John's notes or the Stratosphere's press release), while level 9, from which Levi actually jumped, is either 869 feet high or 866 feet high (depending on whether you trust the Stratosphere's website or the Stratosphere's flyer). So even if you subtract the 4 feet 10 inches that Levi dropped down in order to get to the observation deck's moat, that still leaves a height of about 859 feet from which he would have actually jumped, not 833 feet as the Coroner's Report claims. In fact, in order for him to have jumped from a height of 833 feet, Levi would have had to jump from the 106th floor, which would have been an impossibility, because the 106th floor is occupied by a restaurant called the Top of the World, which is entirely sealed off from the outside by windows. In other words, he couldn't have jumped from that level unless he somehow scaled the plate-glass windows, which still would not have been possible because they're pitched at something like a 70-degree angle. So something's wrong here. And that's not the only problem. The estimate of 5:00 p.m. for Levi leaving his house is extremely improbable. Counting back, for example, let's take the time of his fence-jumping reported by the coroner as 5:58 p.m., which we can confidently assert because it was recorded by the hotel's security camera. (Unless the

internal clock on the camera was wrong, but let's not go there.) For all intents and purposes, then, let's consider this time our end point, when Levi jumps off the building. According to this 5:58 p.m. mark, if Levi were to have left his house at 5:00 p.m., it should have taken him 58 minutes to travel from front door to ledge. Itemizing his trip, we can break it down into a number of segments: (A) from front door to car; (B) from house to parking entrance; C) from parking entrance to parking space; (D) from parking space to casino entrance; (E) from casino entrance to the closest main escalator (if we ignore the nonsensical path traced by John and instead take the shortest route from entrance to elevator) and then up to the ticket booth; (F) from the end of the ticket line until he purchased his tickets; (G) from purchasing his tickets, to walking through the mall, to reaching the end of the line at the bottom of the tower; (H) from the end of the line at the bottom of the tower, through security and the metal detector, up the stairs, and then waiting in line to get on the elevator; (I) from the end of the line to get on the elevator to being on the elevator; (J) from being in the elevator at the bottom of the tower to being in the elevator at the top of the tower; (K) from exiting the elevator at the top of the tower to walking up the stairs and out the door and along the fence. Now, for this time line to be feasible, the sum of the durations of each of these segments must equal 58 minutes. We can effectively ignore John's assertion that Levi parked his car at the Stratosphere at 5:18 p.m. because it is entirely groundless. And neither will we take the publicity manager Michael Gilmartin's estimate in the *Las Vegas Review-Journal* that Levi reached the observation deck at 5:45 p.m., since this is also probably an inexact approximation. So, working backward from 5:58 p.m. (when Levi jumped off the ledge): it probably took Levi about one minute to get from the elevator door to

to the invisible black mountains around it, the wall that would keep the city forever the shape it now was. Security officer Frank then approached Levi from the left, the east, and said "Hey," or he said "Hey, kid," or he said "Kid, no," or he said nothing, and it was his presence alone that caused Levi to turn his head to the left, stand up on the ledge, wave to the security officer, who does not appear on the screen of the video on which Levi is waving, and jump.

the fence. He had to walk out the door, up past the snack bar, up the flight of stairs, out the door, and over to the fence (K = 1 min.). The elevator ride probably took about a minute: (854 feet) * (1 min./1800 feet) * (60 sec./min.) = 28.5 seconds, plus the time it took for the crowded elevator to unload and load at the bottom, and then unload at the top, which would add up to about 1.5 minutes on a good day (J = 1.5 min.). Then he would have had to wait in the hall outside the elevator for probably a good 3–5 minutes, depending on how long the line was. We'll be optimistic and say 3 minutes (I = 3 min.). On a Saturday evening in July during the 5:00–6:00 p.m. hour, we can safely say that the time he would have had to wait in that line, move through the metal detector, and then get to the elevator door must have been at least 40 minutes, given my own experience in the line at a comparable time of day in a comparable season (H = 40 min.). If he walked very briskly, I give him two minutes from the ticket booth to the end of the line at the base of the tower (J = 2 min.) I'd guess another ten minutes at least to buy tickets, again given my own experience (F = 10 min.). From the parking garage exit and casino entrance, down the stairs and escalator, across the casino floor, up the stairs and escalator to the ticket line, 2 minutes (E = 2 min.). If he took the stairs rather than waiting for the elevator, from his primo fifth-floor parking spot, and walked to the casino entrance, 1 minute (D = 1 min.). From the entrance, where he would have had to look for a parking space until he found one on the fifth level, minimum 3 minutes (C = 3 min.). No way in hell, given the godforsaken traffic in that godforsaken city, did it take him the Google Maps-estimated 17 minutes to go 12.6 miles from his house to the casino on an early Saturday night. It probably would have taken him at least twice that long, let's say 35 min., given the likely traffic on the freeway, and let's not even talk about navigating Las Vegas Boulevard (a.k.a "the Strip") on a Saturday night (B = 35 min.). And given that he was mad, and assuming his transmission was good and there were no problems starting his car, from slamming his door to the beginning of his drive, 30 seconds (A = .5 min.). So, adding together A–K, we get 99 minutes, which, subtracted from 5:58, means that the actual time he would have needed to leave his house would have been 4:19 p.m.—39 minutes earlier than his parents claim Levi left their house in their statement to the coroner. Would you forget the time you last saw your child alive? Anything is possible, I suppose, but they don't even seem to have gotten the hour right. The point being that the Presleys' own account now seems questionable, too. And while it is humanly possible that he could have left his house at around 5:00 p.m. (*kind of* close to when they claim Levi left the house) and reached the fence on the Stratosphere's observation deck at 5:58 p.m., it seems incredibly improbable, all things considered. So either there was no traffic on the highway and he hit all the lights and he drove straight to his parking spot and he jogged unerringly from point to point through the casino and every single line he had to wait in was mysteriously short for a Saturday night and he was the first one off the elevator and then went straight to the second level of the observation deck to a predetermined spot along that fence where he immediately began to climb up and immediately then jumped off, and managed to do this all in approximately 58 minutes, or the Coroner's Report, via the report of Levi's parents, is off by a pretty significant amount. So, I guess I have to wonder that if this one fact in the only existing document that officially records Levi Presley's death is this significantly unreliable, to what extent can we trust the reliability of the Coroner's Report as a whole, or the reliability of Levi's parents themselves? Obviously, Levi's parents were in emotional shock when all this went down, so a foggy memory on their part is totally understandable. But how rigorous was the coroner's investigation? Sure, they have to do this 264 times a year for every suicide in Vegas, and there were apparently a number of suicides that weekend. But still, this seems like sloppy work. Did they not even bother doing the math to determine whether their timetable was possible? And if not, then how can we trust the reliability of anything else in this document? Did they also take at their word the statements of the "official" eyewitnesses? And what about the report from the Las Vegas police? Or of all those newspaper reporters? Which of these sources can we trust as "the" authority if they all have demonstrated in one way or another the potential of inaccurately representing what actually happened that night? And at this point, does it even matter? I mean, even if everything that's in question could be verified by unbiased third-party witnesses, and even if I could definitively determine to a fraction of a second exactly when it was that Levi left his house and from how high it was that he jumped and in what direction the wind happened to be blowing—and how hard, and at what temperature, and whether there was dust or not—when he dove off the tower at 6:01:53 p.m, and plummeted for a total of 8 seconds onto a sidewalk of brown-brick herringbone . . . well, then . . . I don't know. I'd have done my job. But wouldn't he still be dead?

Acknowledgments

Deep thanks to our editor, Jill Bialosky, for her faith in this project and for her courage in taking it on. To Alison Liss, for shepherding it into being with remarkable finesse. And to agent Matt McGowan for standing by it from the start.

Thanks as well to John Sullivan, formerly of *Harper's,* who first commissioned the essay upon which this project is based. To Andrew Leland, formerly of *The Believer,* for dealing with the agonizing hassles involved in finally publishing the essay. And most especially to Heidi Julavits, hands down the most generous and ingenious editor of our generation, for grabbing onto the idea of publishing the essay and never letting it go—for seven long years.

Lastly, we both thank Gail and Levi Presley for giving us their blessings to publish this book. Their fearless candor in addressing not only their son's passing but the epidemic of suicide that afflicts Las Vegas is an extraordinary gift—whether or not Las Vegas is yet ready to accept it. They have our respect, and love.

For Levi Presley

Royalties from this book—for the life of its publication—will be donated to a scholarship established in Levi's name at Pino and Bantam ATA Black Belt Academy in Las Vegas, a Tae Kwon Do studio run by Levi's best friend and his best friend's mom. The scholarship will give underprivileged kids in Las Vegas the chance to discover the sport that Levi loved.

About the Authors

John D'Agata teaches creative writing at the University of Iowa in Iowa City, where he lives.

Jim Fingal served for several years as a fact-checker at *The Believer* and *McSweeney's*, where he worked on the titles *What Is the What, Surviving Justice, Voices from the Storm,* and others. He currently lives in Cambridge, Massachusetts, where he designs software.